Financial Freedom

A Beginner's Guide to Stocks and Shares

By: Isaac Banahene Amoyaw

Table of Contents

Chapter 1

Introduction to Stocks and Shares

Understanding the Basics of Stocks

When building wealth and securing a financially stable future, stocks and shares play a crucial role. In this subchapter, we will delve into the fundamentals of stocks, providing you with a foundation of knowledge to navigate the world of finance and investments.

What are Stocks?

Stocks, also known as shares or equities, represent ownership in a company. When you purchase stocks, you become a shareholder, which means you have a claim on the company's assets and earnings. Publicly traded companies typically issue stocks that can be bought and sold on stock exchanges.

Why Invest in Stocks?

Investing in stocks offers numerous advantages. Firstly, stocks have historically provided higher returns than other investment options like bonds or savings accounts. While they may be subject to market volatility, stocks have the potential for long-term growth and capital appreciation.

Furthermore, investing in stocks allows you to become a part-owner of successful companies and benefit from their profits and growth. Stocks also provide liquidity, meaning you can easily convert them into cash whenever needed.

Types of Stocks

There are various types of stocks, each with its characteristics. Common stocks are the most common type and offer voting rights in company decisions. Preferred stocks, conversely, do not provide voting rights but offer a fixed dividend payment.

Understanding Market Indices

Market indices, such as the S&P 500 or the Dow Jones Industrial Average, serve as benchmarks to measure the overall stock market's performance or specific sectors. These indices track a selection of stocks and provide insights into market trends and performance.

Risks and Rewards

Investing in stocks involves risks, including the potential for loss of capital. However, with proper research and diversification, you can manage risks effectively. Understanding market trends, company fundamentals, and economic indicators will help you make informed investment decisions.

Getting Started

To begin investing in stocks, you will need a brokerage account. Choose a reputable broker that offers user-friendly platforms, research tools, and competitive fees. Setting clear investment goals, determining your risk tolerance, and creating a well-diversified portfolio is essential.

Conclusion

Understanding the basics of stocks is essential for anyone interested in achieving financial freedom and building wealth. By investing in stocks, you become a part-owner of successful companies and have the potential to generate significant returns over time. However, conducting thorough research, diversifying your investments, and remaining disciplined in your investment strategy is crucial. With the proper knowledge and approach, stocks can be a powerful tool to help you achieve your financial goals.

Different Types of Shares

In finance, stocks and shares are often used interchangeably to refer to ownership interests in a company. However, it is essential to understand that different types of shares are available in the market, each with unique characteristics and benefits. This subchapter aims to provide a comprehensive overview of the various types of shares one can invest in, empowering readers with the knowledge to make informed investment decisions.

1. Common Shares: Common shares, also known as ordinary shares, are the most common type available in the market. When you buy common shares, you become a partial company owner. As a shareholder,

you have voting rights and may receive dividends based on the company's profitability. However, in the event of liquidation, common shareholders have the lowest priority in receiving their investment back.

2. Preferred Shares: Preferred shares are another type of stock that offers certain advantages over ordinary shares. The primary advantage is that preferred shareholders have a higher claim on the company's assets and earnings. They receive dividends before common shareholders and have a greater chance of recovering their investment in case of bankruptcy. However, preferred shareholders usually do not have voting rights.

3. Growth Shares: Growth shares are issued by companies expected to grow at an above-average rate compared to the broader market. These shares typically do not pay regular dividends but offer potential capital appreciation over time. Growth shares are popular among investors willing to take on more risk in exchange for potentially higher returns.

4. Income Shares: Income shares, also known as dividend shares, are issued by companies that distribute a significant portion of their profits to shareholders in the form of dividends. These shares attract investors seeking a regular income stream from their investments, particularly those nearing retirement or looking for stable cash flow.

5. Blue-Chip Shares: Blue-chip shares refer to stocks of large, well-established, and financially stable companies with a consistent performance history. These companies are often leaders in their respective industries and have a strong record of generating profits. Blue-chip shares are considered relatively less risky than other shares and are favoured by conservative investors.

6. Penny Shares: Penny shares, also known as micro-cap or small-cap shares, are stocks of companies with a small market capitalization. These shares are often priced at a few cents or a few dollars per share. Penny shares are highly speculative and can be subject to significant price volatility. They are popular among investors looking for

potentially high returns but are willing to tolerate higher risk.

Understanding the different types of shares is crucial for any investor looking to build a diversified portfolio. By considering their investment goals, risk tolerance, and time horizon, individuals can decide which types of shares are most suitable for their financial freedom journey.

Benefits of Investing in Stocks

Investing in stocks can benefit individuals looking to grow their wealth and achieve financial freedom. Whether a novice investor or an experienced trader, understanding the advantages of investing in stocks is crucial for achieving your financial goals. This subchapter will explore the key benefits of investing in stocks.

1. Potential for High Returns: One of the primary reasons why people invest in stocks is the potential for high returns. Historically, stocks have outperformed other investment options like bonds or savings accounts over the long term. While the stock market can be volatile in the short term, investing in quality

stocks with a long-term perspective can lead to significant wealth accumulation.

2. Ownership Stake: When you invest in stocks, you become a partial company owner. This ownership allows you to participate in the company's growth and profitability. As the company's value increases, so does the value of your investment. Owning stocks also gives you specific rights, such as voting on important company decisions and receiving dividends, a portion of the company's profits distributed to shareholders.

3. Diversification: Investing in stocks provides an excellent opportunity to diversify your investment portfolio. Investing in stocks from different industries and sectors can spread your risk and reduce the impact of any company's poor performance on your overall portfolio. Diversification helps protect your investments while potentially maximizing returns.

4. Liquidity: Stocks offer high liquidity, meaning you can buy or sell them anytime during market hours. Unlike other investment options, such as real estate or certain bonds, stocks can be easily converted

into cash without much hassle. This liquidity provides flexibility and allows you to respond quickly to changing market conditions or capitalize on investment opportunities.

5. Accessibility: Investing in stocks has become increasingly accessible to the general public. With the rise of online brokerage platforms and investment apps, anyone can start investing in stocks with just a few clicks. Additionally, you can invest in stocks with any budget, as a wide range of companies with different stock prices and market capitalizations are available for investment.

In conclusion, investing in stocks offers several benefits for individuals seeking financial freedom. From the potential for high returns and ownership stake in companies to diversification, liquidity, and accessibility, stocks provide a pathway to grow wealth over time. Understanding these benefits and developing a well-informed investment strategy can help you navigate the stock market and achieve your financial goals.

Risks Associated with Stocks

In finance, stocks and shares have long been considered among the most popular investment options. However, beginners must understand that investing in stocks has a fair share of risks. This subchapter sheds light on the potential dangers associated with stocks, providing valuable insights to general readers and those specifically interested in finance, stocks, and shares.

1. Market Volatility: One of the primary risks associated with stocks is market volatility. Stock prices can fluctuate rapidly, influenced by various factors such as economic conditions, political instability, or company-specific news. These fluctuations can result in significant gains or losses for investors, depending on their timing and decision-making.

2. Economic Downturns: Stocks are highly susceptible to economic downturns, such as recessions or financial crises. During these periods, the overall market sentiment tends to be negative, causing stock prices to decline. Investors need to be prepared for the possibility of a downturn and have strategies in place to mitigate the impact.

3. Company Risk: Investing in individual stocks exposes investors to company-specific risks. These risks include poor management decisions, declining sales, or legal issues. It is crucial to thoroughly research and understand a company's fundamentals before investing, as these risks can significantly impact stock prices.

4. Liquidity Risk: Liquidity risk refers to the difficulty of buying or selling stocks at desired prices due to insufficient market activity. For less actively traded stocks, liquidity risk may be higher, making it challenging to exit positions quickly or at favourable prices.

5. Regulatory and Political Risks: Regulatory changes or political events can significantly impact the stock market. New regulations, trade disputes, or changes in government policies can create uncertainty, which can lead to market volatility and affect stock prices.

6. Psychological Bias: Psychological bias is another risk associated with stock investing. Investors may be influenced by emotions such as fear or greed, leading to irrational decision-making. It is crucial to have a

disciplined approach to investing and avoid making impulsive decisions based on short-term market movements.

While stocks offer the potential for significant returns, it is essential to recognize and manage the risks involved. Diversification, thorough research, and a long-term investment mindset can help mitigate these risks while maximizing the potential benefits of investing in stocks. By understanding and being aware of the risks, investors can make informed decisions and work towards achieving financial freedom.

Importance of Stock Market Analysis

The Importance of Stock Market Analysis

In finance, the stock market is a powerful force that can allow individuals to achieve financial freedom. However, navigating this complex and ever-changing landscape requires a deep understanding of the market and the ability to analyze it effectively. This subchapter highlights the importance of stock market analysis and its role in helping individuals make informed decisions regarding investing in stocks and shares.

Stock market analysis involves examining various factors that can influence the performance of stocks and shares. These factors range from macroeconomic indicators such as GDP growth and interest rates to company-specific information like earnings reports and management decisions. By analyzing these factors, investors can gain valuable insights into a company's prospects and make more informed investment decisions.

One of the critical reasons why stock market analysis is crucial is its ability to help investors identify potential investment opportunities. By studying historical price trends, market patterns, and various technical indicators, analysts can pinpoint stocks that are likely to perform well in the future. This information can be invaluable for investors looking to maximize their returns and build a robust investment portfolio.

Furthermore, stock market analysis is vital in managing risks associated with investing in stocks and shares. Investors can assess an investment's potential risks and rewards by analysing market trends and company fundamentals. This helps identify stocks that offer a favourable risk-to-reward ratio and align with one's investment goals.

Another significant aspect of stock market analysis is its ability to give investors a competitive edge. In today's fast-paced and competitive financial markets, having access to accurate and timely information is crucial. Through in-depth analysis, investors can gain insights that are not readily available to the general public. This allows them to make well-informed decisions ahead of the market, leading to potentially higher returns and reduced risks.

Whether you are a novice or an experienced investor, understanding stock market analysis is essential for achieving financial freedom. It empowers individuals to make informed investment decisions, identify opportunities, manage risks, and gain a competitive advantage. By dedicating time to learning and mastering the art of market analysis, you can position yourself to unlock the full potential of stocks and shares and pave your way toward financial success.

Chapter 2

Getting Started with Stock Market Investing

Setting Financial Goals

One of the most crucial steps in the journey towards financial freedom is setting clear and realistic financial goals. Whether you are a novice or an experienced investor in stocks and shares, having well-defined financial goals provides a roadmap for your financial success. This subchapter will guide you through setting financial goals and their importance in finance, stocks, and shares.

Financial goals act as a compass, directing your efforts and decisions toward achieving your desired economic outcomes. They provide a sense of purpose and motivation, helping you stay focused on your long-term objectives. Without clear goals, measuring progress and determining the necessary steps to reach your financial aspirations becomes challenging.

When setting financial goals, it is essential to consider both short-term and long-term objectives. Short-term goals may include building an emergency fund, paying off debts, or saving for a down payment on a house. Long-term goals, on the other hand, may involve retirement planning, creating a diversified investment portfolio, or funding your child's education.

To ensure your financial goals are attainable, they should be specific, measurable, achievable, relevant, and time-bound (SMART). By following this framework, you can establish realistic and within-reach objectives. For instance, a SMART objective would be saving $10, 000 over the next 12 months by setting aside $800 monthly from your income.

Additionally, it is crucial to review and reassess your financial goals regularly. As your circumstances change, your goals may need adjustment to reflect new priorities, opportunities, or challenges. By evaluating and adapting your goals, you can stay on track and make informed decisions that align with your financial aspirations.

Remember, financial goals should be personal and unique to your situation. What works for someone else may not necessarily work for you. Consider your risk tolerance, time horizon, and financial obligations when determining your goals. Lastly, it is important to celebrate milestones along the way to keep yourself motivated and focused on the path to financial freedom.

Setting financial goals is the foundation of your financial journey. Defining your objectives will give you clarity, direction, and purpose in pursuing financial freedom. Whether you are just starting or have been investing for years, setting financial goals will help you navigate the world of finance, stocks, and shares with confidence and purpose.

Choosing the Right Brokerage Account

In finance, stocks and shares can offer a gateway to achieving financial freedom. However, selecting the proper brokerage account that suits your needs and goals before diving into the exciting investing world is crucial. A brokerage account is a platform to buy and sell securities, and finding the perfect fit can significantly impact your overall investment experience.

When selecting a brokerage account, it is essential to consider several factors. First and foremost, you should evaluate the fees and commissions associated with the account. Different brokerages charge varying amounts, and these costs can significantly eat into your returns over time. Look for a brokerage that offers competitive pricing and consider the types of trades you plan to execute. Some brokerages may charge lower fees for specific transactions, such as online trades or limit orders.

Another critical aspect is the range of investment options available through the brokerage. Ensure the brokerage offers a wide selection of stocks and shares that align with your investment strategy. If you have a specific niche, such as technology or healthcare, ensure that the brokerage provides access to these sectors. Additionally, consider whether the brokerage offers access to other investment vehicles like mutual funds, exchange-traded funds (ETFs), or options if you plan to diversify your portfolio.

The user interface and trading tools the brokerage provides are also crucial considerations. A user-friendly platform with intuitive navigation can significantly enhance your trading experience, especially if you are a beginner. Look for features such as real-time market data, customizable watchlists, and educational resources to help you make informed decisions. Research tools and analysis capabilities can also benefit those looking to delve deeper into the market.

Furthermore, assessing the level of customer support the brokerage provides is essential. Inevitably, questions or issues may arise during your investing journey, and having reliable customer support can be invaluable. Look for brokerages that offer various support channels, such as phone, email, and live chat, and check their reputation for responsiveness and helpfulness.

Ultimately, choosing the correct brokerage account is a personal decision that should be based on your individual preferences and investment goals. Take the time to research and compare different options, considering factors such as fees, investment options, user interface, and customer support. By selecting a brokerage account that aligns with your needs, you can embark on your journey toward financial freedom with confidence and peace of mind.

Opening a Stock Trading Account

Opening a stock trading account is the first step to embark on your journey towards financial freedom through the world of stocks and shares. This subchapter will guide you through the process, ensuring you understand the necessary steps.

A stock trading account is an essential tool that allows you to buy and sell stocks and shares in various companies. It acts as a gateway to the exciting world of the stock market, enabling you to participate in the growth and success of businesses.

The process of opening a stock trading account is relatively straightforward. It would be best if you first decided whether you want to choose a traditional brokerage firm or an online trading platform. Traditional brokerage firms often provide personalized services and advice, while online platforms offer convenience and lower fees. Depending on your preferences, you can select the option that aligns best with your needs.

Once you have decided on the type of firm, you will need to gather the necessary documents. These typically include identification documents, proof of address, and a completed application form. Be sure to have these documents readily available to expedite the account opening process.

After submitting the required documents, you may be prompted to fund your account. This involves depositing an initial amount of money into your stock trading account. The minimum deposit varies depending on the brokerage or platform you choose. It is advisable to start with a conservative amount until you become more comfortable with the stock market.

Once your account is funded, you will receive login details to access your trading platform. Take the time to familiarize yourself with the platform's features, such as market research tools, order placement options, and account management functions. Understanding these tools will help you make informed investment decisions and maximize your potential returns.

Opening a stock trading account is just the beginning of your financial freedom journey. Continuously educate yourself about the stock market, study different investment strategies, and stay updated with the latest market trends. With dedication, patience, and a well-informed approach, you can harness the power of stocks and shares to build a prosperous future.

Whether you aspire to grow wealth, save for retirement, or achieve financial independence, opening a stock trading account is crucial to achieving your goals. Embrace this opportunity, and let the world of stocks and shares pave the way to your financial freedom.

Understanding Stock Market Jargon

In finance, stocks and shares are often the gateway to financial freedom. However, for beginners, the stock market can be a confusing and overwhelming place filled with jargon and complex terms. To navigate this world successfully, it is crucial to have a solid understanding of the stock market jargon. This subchapter aims to demystify the commonly used terms and provide clarity to beginners in finance, stocks, and shares.

One of the most fundamental concepts in the stock market is the stock itself. A stock represents ownership in a company and is divided into shares. These shares are bought and sold on the stock market. To track the performance of the market as a whole, investors often refer to indices like the Dow Jones Industrial Average (DJIA) or the Standard & Poor's 500 Index (S&P 500).

When it comes to buying and selling stocks, investors use brokerage accounts. A brokerage account is a platform a brokerage firm provides that allows investors to execute trades. It is essential to understand different types of orders, such as market orders, limit orders, and stop orders, determining the price at which a trade is executed.

Investors use financial statements such as income, balance, and cash flow to measure a company's profitability. These statements provide insights into a company's revenue, expenses, assets, liabilities, and cash flow.

Valuing a stock is another crucial aspect of investing. Investors use price-to-earnings ratio (P/E ratio), price-to-sales ratio (P/S ratio), and dividend yield to assess whether a stock is undervalued or overvalued.

Understanding market trends is vital for successful investing. Rising stock prices characterize bull markets, while bear markets reflect falling prices. Investors must also be aware of market corrections and crashes, which can significantly impact their investments.

Lastly, knowing about different investment strategies, such as value investing, growth investing, and dividend investing, is essential. These strategies help investors identify stocks that align with their financial goals and risk tolerance.

By familiarizing yourself with this stock market jargon, you will gain the confidence and knowledge to make informed investment decisions. Remember, the stock market is dynamic, and continuous learning is critical to achieving financial freedom in finance, stocks, and shares.

Setting a Budget for Investments

When it comes to investing in stocks and shares, one of the first and most important steps you need to take is setting a budget for your investments. Establishing a budget helps you stay disciplined and organized and ensures that you are making informed decisions about your financial future. This subchapter will explore the key considerations for setting a budget for investments.

The first step in setting a budget is to assess your current financial situation. Take a close look at your income, expenses, and savings. Determine how much disposable income you have available to invest. It is crucial to be realistic and only allocate funds you can comfortably afford to invest without jeopardizing your daily life or emergency savings.

Next, establish your investment goals. Are you looking for short-term gains or long-term wealth accumulation? Your investment goals will influence how much you allocate towards your investments. If you aim for short-term profits, you may need to invest a more significant portion of your budget.

Conversely, if you are focused on long-term wealth accumulation, you can allocate a minor part of your budget and gradually increase it over time.

Another factor to consider is your risk tolerance. Investments inherently involve risk, and different individuals have varying tolerance levels. Assess your risk appetite and adjust your budget accordingly. If you are risk-averse, you may allocate a smaller portion of your budget to higher-risk investments and focus more on safer options. On the other hand, if you are comfortable taking higher risks, you may allocate a more significant portion of your budget to potentially higher-yielding investments.

Additionally, diversification should be a key consideration when setting a budget. Spreading your investments across different asset classes, sectors, and geographical regions can help mitigate risks and maximize potential returns. Allocate your budget to other investment opportunities to ensure a well-diversified portfolio.

Lastly, regularly review and adjust your budget as your financial situation and investment goals change. Periodically assess your income, expenses, and savings to ensure your budget remains realistic and aligned with your objectives.

In conclusion, setting a budget for investments is crucial in your financial journey. By assessing your financial situation, establishing investment goals, considering risk tolerance, practising diversification, and periodically reviewing your budget, you can make informed decisions that align with your financial objectives and help you achieve long-term financial freedom.

Chapter 3

Fundamental Analysis of Stocks

Evaluating Financial Statements

Financial Freedom: A Beginner's Guide to Stocks and Shares

Welcome to the subchapter on evaluating financial statements! This section will delve into the essential skill of analyzing financial statements to make informed decisions in finance, stocks, and shares. Whether you are a general reader or have a specific interest in finance, stocks, and shares, understanding how to evaluate financial statements is paramount to achieving financial success.

Financial statements comprehensively overview a company's financial health and performance. By examining these statements, investors can gain valuable insights into a company's profitability, liquidity, and overall stability. This information is vital when making investment decisions, as it allows you to gauge the potential risks and rewards associated with a particular stock or share.

One crucial aspect of evaluating financial statements is understanding the three primary statements: the income statement, balance sheet, and cash flow statement. The income statement displays a company's revenue, expenses, and net income, while the balance sheet provides a snapshot of a company's assets, liabilities, and shareholders' equity. Lastly, the cash flow statement tracks the cash movement within an organization, including operating, investing, and financing activities.

Examining critical ratios and metrics is essential to evaluate financial statements effectively. These include profitability ratios like return on equity (ROE) and gross profit margin, liquidity ratios such as the current and quick ratios, and leverage ratios like debt-to-equity ratios. You can determine a company's financial strengths and weaknesses by comparing these ratios with industry benchmarks or historical data.

Additionally, scrutinizing the notes to the financial statements is crucial. These notes provide additional context and explanations for the numbers presented in the information. They can highlight any significant events, changes in accounting policies, or contingent liabilities that may impact the company's financial standing.

Lastly, investors should consider the broader economic and industry factors that may influence a company's financial statements. The state of the economy, market trends, and competition can all impact a company's financial performance and should be considered during the evaluation process.

In conclusion, evaluating financial statements is vital for anyone interested in finance, stocks, and shares. By understanding the critical components of financial information, analyzing ratios and metrics, and considering external factors, investors can make informed decisions and increase their chances of achieving financial freedom. So, delve into the world of financial statements and unlock the secrets they hold to embark on your journey to financial success.

Analyzing Company Performance

In finance, understanding how to analyze a company's performance is crucial for making informed investment decisions. The ability to evaluate a company's financial health and predict its prospects can significantly enhance your chances of achieving financial freedom. This subchapter will delve into the various aspects of analyzing company performance, providing you with the essential tools to navigate the complex world of stocks and shares.

One of the critical factors to consider when analyzing a company's performance is its financial statements. These statements, including the balance sheet, income statement, and cash flow statement, provide valuable insights into the company's profitability, liquidity, and overall financial stability. By carefully examining these statements, you can assess the company's revenue growth, profitability margins, debt levels, and cash flow trends. This will help you determine whether the company is on a solid financial footing or if any red flags may warrant caution.

Another crucial aspect of analyzing company performance is evaluating its competitive position within the industry. Understanding the company's market share, customer base, and competitive advantages will give you a clearer picture of its long-term growth potential. Assessing factors such as industry trends, barriers to entry, and the company's ability to innovate will help you determine whether it can maintain its competitive edge in the future.

Additionally, analyzing a company's management team and corporate governance practices is vital. Strong leadership, a clear strategic vision, and effective decision-making are critical indicators of a company's long-term success. By researching the qualifications and track record of the management team, you can gain confidence in their ability to steer the company towards sustainable growth.

Furthermore, it is essential to understand macroeconomic factors and their impact on the company's performance. Factors like interest rates, inflation, and government policies can significantly influence a company's profitability and market conditions. By staying abreast of economic indicators and industry trends, you can better predict how these external factors affect the company's financial performance.

In conclusion, analyzing company performance is critical for anyone seeking financial freedom through stocks and shares. You can make more informed investment decisions by examining financial statements, evaluating competitive positioning, assessing management quality, and considering macroeconomic factors. Remember, thorough analysis and due diligence are crucial to identifying solid investment opportunities and avoiding pitfalls.

Assessing Industry Trends

In finance, staying updated with the latest industry trends is crucial for anyone interested in stocks and shares. Understanding the ever-changing landscape and identifying emerging opportunities can significantly impact financial success. This subchapter aims to equip you with the necessary knowledge and tools to assess industry trends effectively.

Industry trends are patterns and developments observed within specific sectors or markets. By analysing these trends, investors can gain valuable insights into various industries' potential growth, risks, and profitability. Assessing industry trends involves research, data analysis, and informed decision-making.

Staying informed through reliable sources such as financial news outlets, industry reports, and market research is essential when assessing industry trends. These resources provide valuable information about the current state of different sectors, including their performance, challenges, and prospects.

One effective method for assessing industry trends is conducting a SWOT analysis, which stands for strengths, weaknesses, opportunities, and threats. This analysis helps you evaluate the internal and external factors affecting an industry's growth potential. By identifying strengths and options, you can determine which sectors will likely thrive and offer profitable investment opportunities. Conversely, recognizing weaknesses and threats can help you avoid pitfalls and make more informed decisions.

Another valuable approach is to track key performance indicators (KPIs) specific to each industry. KPIs provide quantifiable measurements of different aspects, such as sales growth, market share, profitability ratios, and customer satisfaction. Monitoring these metrics can help you identify industry trends, compare sectors, and make well-informed investment choices.

Furthermore, staying updated with technological advancements and disruptive innovations is crucial. In today's fast-paced world, industries can be heavily influenced by new technologies, changing consumer preferences, and innovative business models. Understanding these trends lets you identify sectors poised for exponential growth and adjust your investment strategies accordingly.

Lastly, networking and engaging with experts in finance, stocks, and shares niches can provide valuable insights into industry trends. Attending industry conferences, joining online forums, and participating in discussions can help you gain knowledge, exchange ideas, and build connections with like-minded individuals.

In conclusion, assessing industry trends is fundamental to successful investing in stocks and shares. You can identify lucrative opportunities and make informed investment decisions by staying informed, conducting thorough research, analyzing key performance indicators, and networking with experts. Remember, the financial landscape is ever-evolving, and adapting to industry trends is crucial for achieving financial freedom.

Understanding Economic Factors

In finance, it is crucial to have a deep understanding of the economic factors that influence the stock market. This subchapter aims to provide a comprehensive overview of these factors, equipping both general readers and those interested in finance, stocks, and shares with the necessary knowledge to navigate this complex landscape.

Economic factors play a significant role in determining the direction of stock prices and overall market trends. As investors, it is essential to stay informed about critical indicators that indicate the health and performance of the economy. This knowledge enables individuals to make informed decisions when buying or selling stocks and shares.

One crucial economic factor is GDP (Gross Domestic Product), which measures the total value of goods and services produced within a country in a specific period. A growing GDP often indicates a healthy economy, leading to increased investor confidence and rising stock prices. Conversely, a decline in GDP may suggest an economic slowdown, causing stock prices to fall.

Another critical economic factor is inflation. Inflation refers to the increase in the prices of goods and services over time. It affects both consumers and investors. High inflation erodes the purchasing power of money, making it essential for investors to consider inflation rates when analyzing potential investments. Central banks often use interest rates to control inflation, making it crucial for investors to monitor changes in these rates.

Unemployment rates also significantly impact the stock market. When unemployment is low, consumer spending tends to increase, leading to higher corporate profits and stock prices. Conversely, high unemployment rates can dampen consumer spending, leading to lower corporate profits and a decline in stock prices.

Additionally, fiscal and monetary policies implemented by governments and central banks substantially impact the economy and, consequently, the stock market. Policies such as tax cuts, government spending, and interest rate adjustments can influence economic growth and investor sentiment.

Understanding economic factors requires continuous monitoring of economic indicators, reading financial reports, and staying informed about global economic trends. By developing a solid grasp of these factors, individuals can make more informed investment decisions and increase their chances of achieving financial freedom.

In conclusion, this subchapter aims to provide a comprehensive understanding of the economic factors that influence the stock market. Whether you are a general reader or have a specific interest in finance, stocks, and shares, this knowledge will prove invaluable in navigating the complex world of investments. By understanding and analyzing economic factors such as GDP, inflation, unemployment rates, and fiscal and monetary policies, investors can make informed decisions, ultimately leading to financial freedom.

Determining Intrinsic Value

Understanding the intrinsic value of stocks and shares is crucial for investors looking to make informed financial decisions. In this subchapter, we will delve into the concept of inherent value and how it can help you assess the true worth of a stock or share.

In essence, intrinsic value represents the actual value of an asset, independent of its market value or current price. It is the value that an asset possesses based on its underlying characteristics, such as its cash flows, earnings potential, and growth prospects. By determining this intrinsic value, investors can identify whether a stock or share is overvalued, undervalued, or reasonably priced.

Various methods can be employed to calculate the intrinsic value of a stock. One such method is fundamental analysis, which involves examining a company's financial statements, competitive position, and industry trends to evaluate its prospects. By analyzing factors like revenue growth, profit margins, and debt levels, investors can estimate a company's future cash flows and discount them back to present value to determine the intrinsic value of its stock.

Another method is relative valuation, which compares a stock's current market price to specific financial ratios or industry benchmarks. This approach helps investors identify whether a stock is trading at a premium or a discount compared to its peers. However, it is essential to consider other factors, such as growth potential, management quality, and market conditions, to assess a stock's intrinsic value comprehensively.

It is worth noting that determining intrinsic value is not an exact science and involves a degree of estimation and judgment. Investors may have different opinions on a stock's inherent worth, leading to varying buy or sell decisions. Therefore, it is crucial to conduct thorough research, employ sound investment principles, and consider multiple valuation methods to arrive at a reasonable estimate of intrinsic value.

Investors can make more informed decisions regarding buying, selling, or holding stocks and shares by determining intrinsic value. This knowledge empowers them to avoid overpaying for assets and identify attractive investment opportunities in the market.

In conclusion, determining intrinsic value is vital for investors in the finance, stocks, and shares niche. It allows them to assess the true worth of a stock or share and make informed investment decisions. By employing various valuation methods, conducting thorough research, and considering multiple factors, investors can estimate the intrinsic value of an asset and make rational choices to achieve financial freedom.

Chapter 4

<hr>

Technical Analysis of Stocks

Introduction to Technical Analysis

In the vast world of finance, understanding the intricacies of the stock market is crucial for anyone seeking financial freedom. One method that has gained immense popularity among investors is technical analysis. Whether you are a beginner in stocks and shares or have some experience, delving into the fascinating realm of technical analysis can significantly enhance your decision-making abilities and increase your chances of success.

Technical analysis is a discipline that examines historical price and volume data to predict future market movements. It is based on the belief that market trends repeat themselves and that studying past price patterns can help identify potential opportunities and risks. By analyzing charts and indicators, technical analysts attempt to forecast the direction of stock prices, aiding investors in making informed decisions.

This subchapter aims to provide a comprehensive introduction to technical analysis, equipping you with the necessary knowledge and tools to navigate the stock market effectively. Regardless of your background or expertise, understanding the principles of technical analysis can prove invaluable in your investment journey.

Throughout this subchapter, we will explore various aspects of technical analysis, starting with the basic concepts and terminology. We will cover essential chart patterns, such as support and resistance levels, trendlines, and moving averages. Additionally, we will delve into the significance of volume and its relationship with price movements.

Furthermore, we will introduce you to various technical indicators, including oscillators, momentum indicators, and moving average convergence divergence (MACD). These indicators are essential for assessing market trends, identifying overbought or oversold conditions, and determining potential entry and exit points.

Lastly, we will discuss the limitations and challenges of technical analysis, as every methodology has its drawbacks. Understanding these limitations will help you develop a well-rounded approach to investing, combining technical analysis with other fundamental and macroeconomic factors.

By the end of this subchapter, you will have a solid foundation in technical analysis, enabling you to interpret and analyze stock market data more effectively. This knowledge will empower you to make informed investment decisions, ultimately helping you achieve financial freedom in stocks and shares.

Whether you are a general reader interested in finance or someone specifically focused on stocks and shares, this subchapter will prove invaluable in your pursuit of financial success. So, let's embark on this exciting journey into technical analysis together!

Chart Patterns and Trends

In finance, understanding chart patterns and trends is crucial for anyone seeking financial freedom through stocks and shares. Whether you are a beginner or have some experience in the field, this subchapter aims to provide a comprehensive overview of chart patterns and trends, enabling you to make informed investment decisions.

Chart patterns are visual representations of historical price movements, offering valuable insights into the future direction of a stock or share. By recognizing these patterns, investors can anticipate potential price movements and adjust their strategies accordingly. Common chart patterns include head and shoulders, double tops and bottoms, triangles, and flags.

Head and shoulders patterns, for instance, indicate a reversal in the stock's current trend. They are characterized by three peaks, with the middle peak being the highest. Identifying this pattern can serve as an indication to sell, as it suggests a downward trend is likely to follow.

On the other hand, double tops and bottoms are reversal patterns that appear when a stock reaches a certain price level twice before reversing its direction. Recognizing these patterns can help investors determine the right time to buy or sell.

Triangles and flags, which are continuation patterns, occur when the stock's price forms a triangle or flag-like shape. These patterns suggest the stock will likely continue its current trend once the consolidation phase ends. Understanding these patterns can assist investors in deciding whether to hold onto their positions or enter new ones.

In addition to chart patterns, understanding trends is equally important. Trends refer to the general direction of a stock's price movement over a certain period. Investors can align their strategies with the market sentiment by identifying the overall trend. Trends can be classified as upward, downward, or sideways, and it is crucial to follow them to maximize potential profits and minimize risks.

Various tools and indicators can be employed to analyze chart patterns and trends effectively. Moving averages, trendlines, and oscillators are commonly used instruments that provide a deeper understanding of price movements. By combining these tools with chart pattern recognition, investors can make well-informed decisions and increase their chances of success in the stock market.

In conclusion, mastering chart patterns and trends is essential for anyone interested in achieving financial freedom through stocks and shares. By understanding these patterns, investors can anticipate potential price movements and adjust their strategies accordingly. Additionally, recognizing trends can help investors align their strategy with the market sentiment, maximizing potential profits. Various tools and indicators can be utilized to analyse these patterns and trends effectively. By combining these tools with chart pattern recognition, investors can make well-informed decisions and increase their chances of success in the dynamic world of stocks and shares.

Support and Resistance Levels

Support and resistance levels are critical concepts in stocks and shares. Understanding these levels can significantly enhance your ability to make informed investment decisions and increase your chances of achieving financial freedom. This subchapter will explore the significance of support and resistance levels, how to identify them, and their practical applications in finance, specifically stocks and shares.

Support levels refer to the price level at which a stock or share tends to find buying support, preventing it from falling further. This level represents a psychological threshold where investors perceive the stock as undervalued, leading to increased demand and price stabilization. Investors can strategically enter or exit positions by identifying support levels, ensuring they capitalize on potential opportunities and mitigate risks.

On the other hand, resistance levels are the opposite of support levels. They represent the price level at which a stock or share faces selling pressure, preventing it from rising further. These levels often act as barriers, as investors perceive the stock to be overvalued, leading to increased supply and price stagnation. Recognizing resistance levels can help investors determine optimal entry and exit points, allowing them to maximize profits and minimize losses.

Identifying support and resistance levels requires combining technical analysis and market observation. Traders often utilize tools like trend lines, moving averages, and chart patterns to locate these crucial levels. By analyzing historical price data and market trends, investors can identify critical levels where buying or selling pressure is likely to occur.

In practice, support and resistance levels can be used in several ways. Investors can use them to set stop-loss orders, protecting their investments from significant losses. They can also utilize these levels to identify potential breakout or breakdown points, which may indicate a change in market sentiment. Additionally, support and resistance levels can act as reference points for determining profit targets and determining the risk-to-reward ratio of a particular investment.

In conclusion, understanding support and resistance levels is essential for anyone seeking financial freedom through stocks and shares. These levels provide valuable insights into market dynamics and can guide investment decisions. Investors can identify critical support and resistance levels by studying historical price data, utilizing technical analysis tools, and observing market trends, enabling them to make more informed and profitable investment choices.

Indicators and Oscillators

Indicators and Oscillators: A Powerful Tool for Analyzing Stocks and Shares

In finance, understanding the dynamics of stocks and shares is essential to achieving financial freedom. Whether you are a seasoned investor or a beginner looking to enter the market, equipping yourself with the proper knowledge and tools is crucial. One device that can significantly enhance your ability to make informed investment decisions is indicators and oscillators.

Indicators and oscillators are valuable analytical tools finance professionals use to assess the health and performance of stocks and shares. They provide valuable insights into market trends, momentum, and potential price reversals, allowing investors to make more accurate predictions.

These tools are handy for beginners looking to build their investment portfolio. Using indicators and oscillators, you can better understand market dynamics, identify potential entry and exit points, and manage your risk effectively.

Various indicators and oscillators are available, each with its unique analysis method. Some common ones include moving averages, Relative Strength Index (RSI), Moving Average Convergence Divergence (MACD), and Bollinger Bands. These tools can be used individually or in combination to generate more comprehensive insights.

Moving averages, for instance, help smooth out price fluctuations and identify trends. They represent whether a stock is in an uptrend, downtrend, or range-bound. Conversely, RSI measures the speed and change of price movements, indicating overbought or oversold conditions. MACD combines moving averages to identify potential momentum shifts, while Bollinger Bands measure volatility and identify potential breakouts.

While indicators and oscillators are powerful tools, it is essential to note that they are not foolproof. They are only as effective as the data and settings used and should be used in conjunction with other forms of analysis. Additionally, market conditions can change rapidly, making it crucial to watch the latest news and developments closely.

In conclusion, indicators and oscillators are invaluable tools for achieving financial freedom through stocks and shares. By utilizing these tools effectively, you can better understand market trends, identify potential opportunities, and manage your risk more efficiently. However, it is essential to remember that these tools are just one piece of the puzzle and should be used with other forms of analysis. So, equip yourself with the knowledge and tools necessary to navigate the world of finance and take a step closer to achieving your financial goals.

Using Technical Analysis Tools

In finance, stocks and shares play a crucial role in wealth creation. However, investing in these instruments requires knowledge and understanding of the market trends and patterns. This is where technical analysis tools come into play. Technical analysis studies historical price and volume data to forecast future market movements. These tools allow investors to make informed decisions and maximize their profits. This subchapter will explore essential technical analysis tools to help beginners in the finance stocks and shares niche achieve financial freedom.

One of the most commonly used technical analysis tools is the moving average. It helps investors identify the average price of a security over a specified period. By comparing the current cost to its moving average, investors can determine if a stock is overbought or oversold and make buying or selling decisions accordingly.

Another powerful tool is the Relative Strength Index (RSI). RSI measures the speed and change of price movements and helps investors identify overbought or oversold conditions. Using RSI, investors can determine whether a stock is due for a price correction or has room for further growth.

Bollinger Bands, developed by John Bollinger, are also widely used in technical analysis. Bollinger Bands consist of a moving average, an upper, and a lower band. The upper and lower bands represent the standard deviation of the stock's price. When the price moves towards the upper band, it indicates that the stock is overbought, and when it moves towards the lower band, it suggests an oversold condition.

Additionally, candlestick charts are a visual representation of price movements. They provide valuable information about a stock's opening, closing, and high and low prices within a specific period. Investors can identify potential reversals or continuations in price trends by analysing candlestick patterns.

While technical analysis tools can provide valuable insights, it is essential to note that they should not be used in isolation. It is advisable to combine technical analysis with fundamental analysis, which involves evaluating a company's financial health, management, and competitive positioning.

In conclusion, mastering technical analysis tools is essential for anyone seeking financial freedom in stocks and shares. Moving averages, RSI, Bollinger Bands, and candlestick charts are just a few examples of the tools available. By effectively understanding and utilizing these tools, investors can make informed decisions and increase their chances of success in the finance stocks and shares niche.

Chapter 5

—◆●◆—

Building a Diversified Stock Portfolio

Importance of Diversification

In finance, one of the most crucial concepts investors need to understand is the importance of diversification. Whether you are a seasoned investor or just starting, diversifying your investment portfolio is vital to achieving long-term financial success. This subchapter will delve into the significance of diversification and how it can benefit individuals in the realm of stocks and shares.

Diversification refers to spreading your investments across various asset classes, sectors, and geographic regions. It is a risk management strategy that aims to minimize the potential negative impact of any single investment on your overall portfolio. By diversifying, you can reduce your exposure to the inherent risks of investing in a single stock or a specific industry.

One of the primary advantages of diversification is the potential to enhance your returns while lowering your portfolio's volatility. By investing in a range of assets, you can potentially benefit from the positive performance of some while offsetting any losses with others. This strategy helps smooth out the fluctuations in your portfolio's value, making it more stable.

Furthermore, diversification allows you to tap into different market opportunities. Other sectors and regions often experience varying levels of growth or decline. By diversifying your investments, you can take advantage of potential growth in emerging markets while benefiting from the stability of more established industries.

Another crucial aspect of diversification is its ability to protect investments against unforeseen events and market downturns. When you diversify, you reduce the impact of any single stock or sector performing poorly. If one investment underperforms, the positive performance of others can help offset those losses, thereby reducing the overall risk to your portfolio.

It is important to note that diversification does not guarantee profits or eliminate all risks associated with investing. However, it is a fundamental strategy that can help investors navigate the unpredictable nature of the stock market and increase their chances of long-term financial success.

In conclusion, diversification is essential to investing in stocks and shares. By spreading your investments across different asset classes, sectors, and regions, you can enhance your returns, reduce portfolio volatility, and protect your investments against market downturns. Understanding the importance of diversification and implementing it in your investment strategy is crucial for achieving financial freedom.

Selecting Stocks for a Balanced Portfolio

A balanced portfolio is crucial in achieving financial freedom through stocks and shares. It requires careful consideration and a systematic approach to ensure optimal returns while minimizing risks. This subchapter will explore the key factors to consider when selecting stocks for a balanced portfolio.

Diversification is the cornerstone of a balanced portfolio. Investing in various stocks across different sectors and industries can reduce the impact of market fluctuations on your overall portfolio. This way, if one industry faces a downturn, other sectors may outperform, offsetting potential losses. The goal is to spread investments across various asset classes, such as large-cap stocks, small-cap stocks, international stocks, and even bonds, to achieve a more stable and resilient portfolio.

Another vital aspect of stock selection is conducting thorough research. Instead of relying solely on hearsay or market trends, take the time to analyze a company's financial health, industry prospects, and growth potential. Look for companies with a solid track record, sustainable competitive advantages, and a clear growth strategy. Additionally, consider their valuation metrics, such as price-to-earnings ratio and dividend yield, to determine if the stock is reasonably priced.

Risk tolerance is another critical factor to consider when selecting stocks. Determine your risk appetite and align it with your investment goals. More aggressive investors may be comfortable with higher-risk, high-growth stocks, while conservative investors prefer stable dividend-paying stocks. Balancing risk and reward is crucial to ensure your portfolio aligns with your financial objectives and comfort level.

Furthermore, staying updated with the latest market trends and news is essential. Regularly monitor your portfolio's performance and make adjustments if necessary. Keep an eye on economic indicators, geopolitical events, and industry-specific information that could impact your stocks. While it is essential to be well-informed, avoid making knee-jerk reactions to short-term market fluctuations. Instead, focus on the long-term potential of your investments.

Investing in stocks and shares involves risks; no investment strategy can guarantee profits. However, by selecting stocks for a balanced portfolio, diversifying your investments, conducting thorough research, aligning risk tolerance, and staying informed, you can increase the likelihood of achieving financial freedom through stocks and shares.

In conclusion, selecting stocks for a balanced portfolio is a critical step toward financial freedom. By diversifying your investments, conducting thorough research, aligning risk tolerance, and staying informed, you can build a resilient portfolio that maximizes returns while minimizing risks. Investing in stocks and shares requires patience, discipline, and a long-term perspective. With the right approach, you can navigate the complex world of finance stocks and shares and work towards achieving your financial goals.

Allocating Capital Effectively

In finance, one of the most vital skills to master is allocating capital effectively. Whether a novice investor or an experienced trader, understanding how to give your funds wisely can make all the difference in achieving financial freedom. This subchapter aims to demystify this concept and provide actionable insights to maximize your returns in stocks and shares.

When investing, the key is picking the right stocks or shares and determining how much capital to allocate to each investment. This process involves careful analysis and consideration of various factors, such as risk tolerance, investment goals, and market conditions.

First and foremost, it is crucial to diversify your portfolio. By spreading your capital across different sectors, industries, and asset classes, you can reduce the impact of any single investment's poor performance. This mitigates the risk of losing all your capital in one fell swoop and increases the potential for long-term growth. Remember the adage, "Don't put all your eggs in one basket. "

Furthermore, conducting thorough research and due diligence before allocating capital is essential. Stay informed about market trends, economic indicators, and company-specific news. This knowledge will enable you to make informed decisions and identify potential investment opportunities.

Another crucial aspect of effective capital allocation is risk management. Assess your risk tolerance level and align it with your chosen investment strategy. High-risk investments may offer the potential for significant returns, but they also come with a higher chance of loss. On the other hand, low-risk investments may provide stability but might not generate substantial profits. Finding the right balance is critical to achieving your financial goals while managing risk effectively.

Regularly reviewing and rebalancing your portfolio is also essential. As market conditions change, some investments may perform better than others, causing your portfolio to become unbalanced. Reallocating capital to underperforming assets or taking profits from overperforming ones ensures that your portfolio aligns with your investment strategy.

In conclusion, allocating capital effectively is a fundamental skill for anyone venturing into the world of stocks and shares. By diversifying your portfolio, conducting thorough research, managing risk, and regularly reviewing your investments, you can enhance your chances of achieving financial freedom. Remember, successful investors are not just lucky; they make intelligent decisions based on careful analysis and strategic capital allocation.

Rebalancing and Adjusting the Portfolio

In the world of finance, maintaining a well-balanced and diversified investment portfolio is crucial for long-term success. This subchapter will delve into the importance of rebalancing and adjusting your portfolio, highlighting its benefits to your financial freedom journey.

Rebalancing your portfolio involves realigning your investments to match your desired asset allocation. Over time, market fluctuations can cause your portfolio to become imbalanced. Some investments may outperform others, leading to a higher concentration of certain assets. By rebalancing, you ensure that your portfolio aligns with your investment goals and risk tolerance.

One of the primary benefits of rebalancing is risk management. When certain investments perform exceptionally well, they may start to dominate your portfolio, exposing you to increased risk. Rebalancing allows you to trim these overperforming investments and redistribute the proceeds into underperforming ones, effectively reducing risk and bringing your portfolio back to its intended allocation.

Moreover, rebalancing helps you take advantage of market opportunities. By selling high-performing investments, you can lock in profits and invest in assets that may be undervalued or have growth potential. This strategy allows you to buy low and sell high, aligning with the age-old wisdom of successful investing.

Adjusting your portfolio goes beyond rebalancing and involves making strategic changes to your asset allocation based on market conditions, economic factors, and financial goals. Regular portfolio evaluation is essential to ensure it remains aligned with your investment strategy.

When adjusting your portfolio, it is crucial to consider your risk tolerance, time horizon, and investment objectives. A well-thought-out adjustment can help you optimize your portfolio and position yourself to capitalize on changing market trends.

In conclusion, rebalancing and adjusting your portfolio is critical in achieving financial freedom through stocks and shares.

By periodically reviewing and realigning your investments, you reduce risk, take advantage of market opportunities, and stay on track toward your financial goals. Remember, effective portfolio management is not a one-time task but a continuous process that requires diligence and adaptability.

Whether you are a beginner or an experienced investor, understanding the importance of rebalancing and adjusting your portfolio is essential. By implementing these strategies, you can confidently navigate the unpredictable world of finance and increase your chances of achieving long-term success.

Long-Term Investing Strategies

When building wealth and achieving financial freedom, long-term investing is a critical strategy that should not be overlooked. This subchapter will explore the various long-term investing strategies to help you grow wealth and navigate the exciting world of stocks and shares.

One of the most essential principles of long-term investing is patience. Unlike short-term trading, long-term investing involves holding onto your investments for an extended period, typically years or even decades. By doing so, you can take advantage of the power of compounding and ride out the inevitable market fluctuations.

Diversification is another crucial strategy for long-term investors. Spreading your investments across different stocks, sectors, and asset classes can help mitigate risk and protect your portfolio from sudden downturns. It is essential to conduct thorough research and consider factors such as company fundamentals, industry trends, and economic indicators before making investment decisions.

Investing in dividend-paying stocks is often favoured by long-term investors. Dividends are a portion of a company's profits distributed to shareholders, providing a regular income stream. By reinvesting these dividends, you can harness the power of compounding and accelerate your wealth accumulation over time.

Another popular long-term investing strategy is dollar-cost averaging. This approach involves regularly investing a fixed amount of money into a particular stock or fund, regardless of market conditions. By doing so, you can take advantage of market fluctuations and potentially buy more shares when prices are low and fewer when prices are high.

Long-term investors should also consider staying informed and regularly reviewing their investment portfolio. Keep track of company news, financial reports, and market trends to make informed decisions and adjust your investments accordingly. However, avoiding knee-jerk reactions based on short-term market fluctuations is essential, as these can often lead to poor investment choices.

In conclusion, long-term investing strategies provide a solid foundation for achieving financial freedom. By practising patience, diversifying your portfolio, investing in dividend-paying stocks, utilizing dollar-cost averaging, and staying informed, you can build wealth over time and confidently navigate the volatile world of stocks and shares. Building wealth is a journey, not a sprint, and adopting a long-term investing mindset is critical to reaching your financial goals.

------ ◆●◆ ------

Chapter 6

Risk Management in Stock Market Investing

Understanding Market Volatility

Market volatility is fundamental in finance, particularly in stocks and shares. It refers to the rapid and significant price fluctuations in financial markets. Whether you are a seasoned investor or just starting, understanding market volatility is crucial for achieving financial freedom.

Various factors, including economic events, political uncertainties, and investor sentiment, can cause volatility. These factors can significantly impact the supply and demand dynamics in the market, resulting in price swings. It is important to note that market volatility is a typical and inherent characteristic of financial markets. However, it can create both opportunities and risks for investors.

One key aspect of understanding market volatility is that it is not synonymous with risk. While high volatility can lead to potential losses, it also presents profit opportunities. Volatile markets provide the chance to buy undervalued stocks and shares at low prices, with the potential for significant returns when the market stabilizes.

To navigate market volatility effectively, it is essential to have a well-diversified portfolio. Diversification involves spreading your investments across different asset classes, sectors, and geographic regions. By diversifying, you can reduce the impact of market volatility on your overall portfolio. This strategy lets you capture gains in certain investments while mitigating losses in others.

Additionally, it is crucial to adopt a long-term perspective when dealing with market volatility. Short-term market fluctuations should not deter you from your investment goals. By focusing on the long-term performance of your investments, you can ride out the ups and downs of the market and potentially benefit from compounding returns.

Furthermore, understanding market volatility requires staying informed and conducting thorough research. Keep up with financial news, economic indicators, and industry trends. This knowledge will help you make informed decisions and identify opportunities amid market turbulence.

In conclusion, market volatility is integral to the finance world, especially stocks and shares. While it may be unsettling, understanding and embracing market volatility can lead to financial freedom. By diversifying your portfolio, maintaining a long-term perspective, and staying informed, you can navigate market volatility effectively and potentially capitalize on its opportunities. Remember, patience and discipline are vital to achieving success in the ever-changing landscape of financial markets.

Setting Stop Loss Orders

One of the most essential techniques successful traders use in financing stocks and shares is setting stop-loss orders. Stop-loss orders act as a safety net, protecting your investment from significant losses if the market turns unexpectedly. This subchapter will delve into stop-loss orders and why they are crucial for achieving financial freedom in the stock market.

A stop-loss order is an automatic instruction to sell a security when it reaches a predetermined price. Setting a stop-loss order establishes a willingness to accept a loss and exit the trade. This technique allows you to limit the potential downside of your investment and protect your capital.

The primary benefit of setting stop-loss orders is that they help you avoid emotional decision-making. In the fast-paced world of stocks and shares, it is easy to get caught up in the excitement or panic of market fluctuations. By predefining your exit point, you remove the emotions from the equation and make rational decisions based on your predetermined strategy.

When setting a stop loss order, it is essential to consider your risk tolerance and the volatility of the stock you are trading. A general rule of thumb is to set the stop loss order at a level that limits your potential loss to no more than 2-3% of your total investment. This ensures your losses remain manageable even if the market moves against you.

Another essential aspect to consider when setting stop-loss orders is to give your investment enough room to breathe. Placing your stop loss order too close to the current market price may lead to unnecessary triggering of the order due to average market volatility. On the other hand, setting it too far away may result in significant losses if the market suddenly reverses.

To make the most effective use of stop-loss orders, it is crucial to regularly monitor your investments and adjust your stop-loss levels as the market conditions change. As the stock price rises, you can consider raising your stop loss order to lock in profits and protect your gains.

In conclusion, setting stop-loss orders is essential for anyone seeking financial freedom to finance stocks and shares. By predefining your exit strategy, you protect your investments from significant losses and make rational decisions based on your predetermined risk tolerance. Regularly monitor and adjust your stop loss levels to adapt to changing market conditions.

Implementing Hedging Strategies

Hedging strategies are an integral part of the world of finance, particularly for those involved in stocks and shares. These strategies allow investors to manage risks and protect their investments in an ever-fluctuating market. This subchapter will explore the different hedging strategies and discuss how they can be effectively implemented.

One common hedging strategy is known as portfolio diversification. This involves spreading investments across different asset classes, industries, and geographical regions. By diversifying their portfolio, investors can reduce the impact of market volatility on their overall returns. For example, if one sector experiences a downturn, the investor's losses can be offset by gains in other sectors.

Another popular hedging strategy is options trading. Options give investors the right, but not the obligation, to buy or sell a specific asset at a predetermined price within a specified timeframe. This allows investors to protect their investments against potential losses by purchasing put options, which give them the right to sell an asset at a predetermined price. On the other hand, investors can also use call options to protect against potential price increases by giving them the right to buy an asset at a predetermined price.

Futures contracts are also commonly used in hedging strategies. A futures contract is an agreement between two parties to buy or sell an asset at a predetermined price on a specific date in the future. By entering into a futures contract, investors can lock in the price of an asset and protect themselves against potential price fluctuations.

It is important to note that while hedging strategies can effectively manage risks, they also come with challenges. For instance, implementing hedging strategies requires a thorough understanding of the market and the various instruments available. Additionally, investors must carefully consider the costs associated with these strategies, such as transaction fees and premiums.

In conclusion, implementing hedging strategies is crucial for investors in finance, particularly in stocks and shares. These strategies offer a way to manage risks and protect investments in an unpredictable market. By diversifying portfolios, engaging in options trading, or utilizing futures contracts, investors can effectively mitigate potential losses and enhance their chances of achieving financial freedom. However, it is essential to carefully analyze and understand the costs and complexities associated with these strategies before implementing them.

Managing Emotions and Avoiding Impulsive Decisions

Managing emotions and avoiding impulsive decisions is crucial for achieving financial freedom in the fast-paced world of finance stocks and shares. Emotions can often cloud judgment and lead to irrational decision-making, harming your investment portfolio. This subchapter aims to equip you with the necessary tools to stay grounded, make informed choices, and navigate the unpredictable nature of the stock market.

1. Understanding the Role of Emotions:

Emotions such as fear, greed, and excitement can significantly influence your investment decisions. By recognizing and acknowledging these emotions, you can take steps to mitigate their impact. Understanding the psychological aspect of investing will help you make rational choices based on logic and analysis.

2. Developing a Trading Plan:

A well-defined trading plan is essential for managing emotions and avoiding impulsive decisions. This plan should include your investment goals, risk tolerance, and a clear strategy for buying and selling stocks. By sticking to a plan, you can avoid making impulsive decisions based on short-term market fluctuations.

3. Practicing Patience and Discipline:

Patience and discipline are virtues that every investor should possess. Embracing a long-term perspective and resisting the urge to react to every market movement will prevent you from making hasty decisions. Remember, successful investing is a marathon, not a sprint.

4. Conducting Thorough Research:

Knowledge is power in the world of finance stocks and shares. Conducting thorough research on companies, sectors, and market trends will help you make informed decisions. By arming yourself with facts and data, you can approach investing with confidence and reduce the influence of emotions.

5. Seeking Professional Advice:

Even the most seasoned investors seek guidance from financial advisors or industry experts. Seeking professional advice can provide valuable insights and help you make objective decisions. However, choosing a reputable advisor who aligns with your financial goals and values is essential.

6. Learning from Past Mistakes:

Mistakes are an inevitable part of investing. However, they can serve as valuable learning experiences. Reflecting on past decisions and analyzing what went wrong will help you avoid repeating the same mistakes in the future. By learning from your mistakes, you can grow as an investor and make better-informed choices.

In conclusion, managing emotions and avoiding impulsive decisions are critical skills for achieving financial freedom in finance stocks and shares. You can become a more successful investor by understanding the role of emotions, developing a trading plan, practising patience and discipline, conducting thorough research, seeking professional advice, and learning from past mistakes. Staying calm and rational during turbulent times is the key to long-term financial success.

Continuously Monitoring and Evaluating Investments

Investing in stocks and shares is a well-known avenue for wealth creation and financial freedom. However, merely investing in these assets is not enough; one must continuously monitor and evaluate one's investments to ensure optimal returns and mitigate potential risks. This subchapter provides a beginner's guide to effectively monitoring and evaluating assets, catering to a general audience interested in finance, stocks, and shares.

Monitoring investments involves keeping a close eye on the performance of individual stocks and the overall market trends. It is essential to stay updated with current events, economic indicators, and industry news that may impact the value of your investments.

Regularly reviewing financial statements, company reports, and analyst recommendations can provide valuable insights into your invested companies' financial health and prospects.

Evaluating investments goes beyond monitoring performance and requires a deeper analysis of various factors. One crucial aspect is assessing the valuation of stocks. Understanding concepts such as price-to-earnings ratio, price-to-book ratio, and dividend yield can help determine whether a stock is overvalued or undervalued. Additionally, evaluating a company's competitive advantage, management team, and growth potential can aid in identifying lucrative investment opportunities.

Diversification is another critical consideration when monitoring and evaluating investments. Spreading your investments across various sectors, industries, and geographical regions can help mitigate risks and minimize the impact of any individual stock's poor performance on your overall portfolio. Regularly rebalancing your portfolio by adjusting the allocation of your investments can ensure that it remains aligned with your risk tolerance and investment goals.

Furthermore, monitoring and evaluating investments also entails a comprehensive understanding of risk management. This involves setting realistic expectations, defining an investment horizon, and incorporating risk-reducing strategies such as stop-loss orders or trailing stops. A clear exit strategy in case an investment underperforms is vital to safeguarding your capital.

In conclusion, continuously monitoring and evaluating investments is essential to achieving financial freedom through stocks and shares. Investors can maximise their returns and minimise potential losses by staying informed, considering valuation, diversifying, and managing risks. Investing is a long-term endeavour, and consistent monitoring and evaluation are crucial to building a successful and resilient investment portfolio.

Chapter 7

Advanced Stock Market Strategies

Value Investing Techniques

In finance, stocks and shares have always been an attractive investment avenue. However, the key to successful investing lies in adopting the right strategies. One such approach that has proven adequate time and again is value investing. This subchapter will delve into the various techniques associated with value investing and highlight their significance for individuals aiming to achieve financial freedom.

Value investing, popularized by legendary investor Benjamin Graham, focuses on identifying undervalued stocks that have the potential to generate substantial returns over the long term. The essence of this approach lies in purchasing stocks at a price lower than their intrinsic value, taking advantage of the market's tendency to undervalue certain companies. By doing so, investors aim to profit from the eventual correction of market prices as the actual value of the stocks becomes recognized by the market.

One of the fundamental techniques employed in value investing is fundamental analysis. This involves evaluating a company's financial health, including revenue growth, profitability, debt levels, and competitive advantages. By thoroughly researching these factors, investors can gauge the company's intrinsic value and determine whether the stock is undervalued or overvalued.

Another important technique is called margin of safety. This concept emphasizes the importance of buying stocks at a significant discount to their intrinsic value. By doing so, investors create a buffer against potential losses and increase their chances of generating substantial returns. A wide margin of safety provides a cushion against unforeseen market volatility or company-specific risks, reducing the overall risk associated with the investment.

Furthermore, value investors often focus on long-term investment horizons. Patience is a virtue in value investing, as it may take time for the market to recognize the actual value of a stock. By holding onto undervalued stocks for an extended period, investors increase their chances of capitalizing on the market's correction and realizing significant gains.

Lastly, diversification is a critical element of value investing. By spreading investments across different industries and sectors, investors minimize the impact of any single stock's poor performance on their overall portfolio. This strategy helps to mitigate risk and maximize potential returns.

In conclusion, value investing techniques offer a compelling approach for individuals seeking financial freedom through stocks and shares. Adopting fundamental analysis, seeking a margin of safety, maintaining a long-term perspective, and diversifying investments are all integral components of successful value investing. By mastering these techniques, investors can identify undervalued stocks, create a well-balanced portfolio, and increase their chances of generating substantial returns in the dynamic world of finance.

Growth Investing Strategies

In the world of finance, stocks and shares present a multitude of opportunities for individuals to grow their wealth. One such approach that has gained popularity among investors is growth investing. This subchapter will delve into the various growth investing strategies, equipping general readers and finance enthusiasts with the knowledge to make informed investment decisions.

As the name suggests, growth investing focuses on investing in companies with strong potential for future growth. The primary goal is to identify stocks of companies that are expected to experience significant increases in revenue, earnings, and market share over time. This strategy is often preferred by those willing to take on a higher level of risk in exchange for potentially higher returns.

One key strategy within growth investing is investing in emerging sectors or industries. These industries are typically in the early stages of development, offering significant growth potential. By identifying emerging sectors, investors can capitalize on the growth opportunities of innovative companies operating within these industries.

Another growth investing strategy involves identifying companies with a competitive advantage or a unique market position. These companies have characteristics that set them apart, such as proprietary technology, strong brand recognition, and a large customer base. Investing in such companies can lead to substantial growth as they dominate their respective markets.

Furthermore, growth investors often focus on companies with a track record of consistent revenue and earnings growth. These companies have demonstrated their ability to increase profits over time, indicating their potential for sustained growth. By analyzing a company's financial statements and performance metrics, investors can identify those that meet their growth criteria.

It is important to note that growth investing requires a long-term perspective. As the saying goes, "Rome wasn't built in a day. " Similarly, significant growth in a company's stock price may take time. Therefore, investors should be patient and allow their investments to grow over a longer time horizon, often years rather than months.

To summarize, growth investing is a strategy that aims to identify companies with significant growth potential. By investing in emerging sectors, companies with a competitive advantage, and those with a track record of consistent growth, investors can position themselves to benefit from the future success of these companies. However, it is crucial to remember that growth investing requires patience and a long-term perspective.

Dividend Investing Opportunities

Dividing is one of the most popular strategies when investing in stocks and shares. Dividends are regular payments companies make to their shareholders to distribute a portion of their profits. This subchapter will delve into dividend investing, its benefits, and how to capitalize on these opportunities to achieve financial freedom.

Dividend investing offers several advantages that make it an attractive option for investors. Firstly, it provides a steady stream of income. Unlike relying solely on capital appreciation, which can be unpredictable, dividends offer a reliable income stream that can be reinvested or used for personal expenses. This stability is especially beneficial for retirees or those seeking passive income.

Furthermore, dividend investing allows investors to take advantage of compounding. By reinvesting dividends back into the stock, you can buy more shares, which leads to an increase in future dividend payments. Over time, this compounding effect can significantly boost your returns, accelerating your journey toward financial freedom.

Dividend investing also provides a level of stability during market downturns. While stock prices may fluctuate, dividend payments tend to be more consistent, providing a cushion during turbulent times. This aspect makes dividend stocks attractive for risk-averse investors looking to balance their portfolios.

To identify dividend investing opportunities, it is crucial to analyze the financial health of companies. Look for stable and established companies with a history of consistently paying dividends. Check their dividend yield, the annual dividend payment divided by the stock price, to determine the potential return on your investment. However, remember that a high dividend yield may indicate an undervalued stock or financial distress, so conduct thorough research.

Dividend investing is not limited to individual stocks. You can also explore dividend-focused exchange-traded funds (ETFs) or mutual funds, which offer diversification by investing in a basket of dividend-paying stocks. This approach mitigates the risk of investing in a single company while reaping the benefits of dividend income.

In conclusion, dividend investing presents a compelling opportunity for investors seeking financial freedom. By focusing on stable companies with a history of dividend payments, you can enjoy a consistent income stream, take advantage of compounding, and find stability in uncertain markets. Whether through individual stocks or dividend-focused funds, dividend investing can be a valuable addition to your investment strategy, helping you achieve long-term financial goals.

Momentum Trading Approaches

In finance, stocks and shares can offer great opportunities for individuals seeking financial freedom. However, navigating the complex world of stock trading can be daunting, especially for beginners. This subchapter, titled "Momentum Trading Approaches, " aims to comprehensively understand this particular trading strategy and how it can be utilized to maximize profits.

Momentum trading is a popular approach among seasoned investors and traders. It capitalizes on the concept that stocks performing well in the past are likely to continue their upward trend, while underperforming stocks are likely to continue their downward trend. This strategy is based on riding the momentum of a stock's price movement rather than trying to predict future trends.

One of the critical aspects of momentum trading is identifying stocks with strong price momentum. Traders often employ technical analysis techniques, such as studying moving averages, chart patterns, and volume indicators, to identify stocks experiencing significant price movements. By focusing on stocks already trending, momentum traders aim to take advantage of the market's current momentum and join the upward or downward trend.

To successfully employ momentum trading, it is crucial to have a well-defined entry and exit strategy. Traders should set clear profit targets and stop-loss orders to protect their investments. It is important to remember that momentum trading requires active monitoring of stock prices and market trends, as positions may need to be adjusted quickly to capitalize on changing market conditions.

While momentum trading can be highly profitable, it is not without risks. Stocks performing well may experience sudden reversals, and market timing is always challenging. Therefore, it is recommended to combine momentum trading with other strategies, such as fundamental analysis, to make informed investment decisions.

In conclusion, momentum trading is a popular approach in stocks and shares. By identifying stocks with strong price momentum and riding the market's current trends, traders can potentially achieve significant profits. However, this trading strategy requires careful analysis, active monitoring, and a well-defined exit strategy to mitigate risks. By combining momentum trading with other strategies, investors can enhance their chances of financial freedom through stock trading.

Options and Futures Trading

In finance, options and futures trading significantly offer investors a wide range of opportunities to maximize their returns and manage their risks. This subchapter aims to provide a comprehensive understanding of options and futures trading for individuals interested in stocks and shares.

Options trading is a popular method that allows investors to buy or sell assets at a predetermined price within a specific timeframe. It offers flexibility and leverage, enabling traders to make substantial profits with limited capital. Options can be used for various purposes, such as hedging against potential losses, generating income through premiums, or speculating on the future movement of an underlying asset.

On the other hand, futures trading involves agreeing to buy or sell an asset at a predetermined price and date in the future. It allows investors to speculate on the price movements of various commodities, indices, or currencies without owning the underlying asset. Futures contracts are standardized, traded on regulated exchanges, and offer high liquidity, making them suitable for short-term and long-term investment strategies.

Before venturing into this exciting field, understanding the basics of options and futures trading is essential. It is crucial to grasp concepts such as call and put options, strike price, expiration date, and the factors influencing the value of these derivatives. Learning about margin requirements, contract specifications, and various trading strategies will empower individuals to make informed investment decisions.

Options and futures trading also come with inherent risks. As with any investment, there is potential loss, and it is essential to carefully assess the risks involved before committing capital. Furthermore, using leverage amplifies potential gains and losses, making risk management a crucial aspect of successful trading.

Individuals must open an account with a reputable brokerage firm for options and futures trading. These firms provide the tools, platforms, and educational resources to assist traders in executing trades effectively. It is essential to conduct thorough research and select a brokerage that aligns with personal trading goals and offers competitive pricing and customer support.

In conclusion, options and futures trading present exciting investor opportunities in stocks and shares. By understanding the fundamentals, managing risks, and selecting the right brokerage, individuals can confidently navigate this field and work towards achieving financial freedom. Knowledge and continuous learning are crucial to success in options and futures trading.

Chapter 8

◆•◆

Financial Planning for Stock Market Investors

Setting Realistic Expectations

When investing in stocks and shares, it is crucial to set realistic expectations. Many people are drawn to the stock market because of the potential for high returns, but it is essential to remember that investing involves risks and uncertainties. This subchapter will provide valuable insights on how to set realistic expectations and avoid common pitfalls in finance stocks and shares.

First and foremost, it is essential to understand that the stock market is unpredictable. While it is possible to achieve significant gains, it is equally likely to experience losses. Stocks and shares are subject to market fluctuations, and even the most experienced investors cannot accurately predict the future performance of individual stocks or the market as a whole. Therefore, it is essential to approach investing with a long-term perspective.

Secondly, before diving into the market, educating yourself about stocks and shares is crucial. Understanding how the stock market works, different investment strategies, and analyzing financial statements will help you make informed decisions. Take the time to research and learn from reputable sources, attend seminars or webinars, and consider consulting with a financial advisor who specializes in stocks and shares. This knowledge will allow you to set realistic expectations and navigate the market more effectively.

Additionally, it is essential to assess your risk tolerance and financial goals. Investing in stocks and shares involves a degree of risk, and evaluating how much risk you are willing to take is crucial. Your risk tolerance will influence the types of stocks and shares you invest in and your investment strategy. Moreover, setting clear financial goals will help you determine how much you need to support and for how long.

Lastly, avoiding falling into the trap of chasing quick gains or trying to time the market is essential. Investing in stocks and shares is a long-term endeavour, and trying to make quick profits can often lead to poor decision-making and increased risk. Instead, focus on building a diversified portfolio, staying disciplined, and being patient. Remember, successful investing is about consistent and disciplined actions over time rather than trying to beat the market in the short term.

In conclusion, setting realistic expectations is crucial when investing in stocks and shares. The stock market is unpredictable, and investing with a long-term perspective is essential, as well as educating yourself, assessing your risk tolerance and financial goals, and avoiding chasing quick gains. By following these principles, you will be better equipped to navigate the world of finance stocks and shares and increase your chances of achieving financial freedom.

Creating a Personal Budget

In "Financial Freedom: A Beginner's Guide to Stocks and Shares, " creating a personal budget is one of the most crucial steps towards achieving financial independence. A personal budget is a powerful tool allowing individuals to control their finances, manage expenses, and ultimately achieve their financial goals. Whether you are new to finance or an experienced investor in stocks and shares, understanding how to create a personal budget is essential.

The first step in creating a personal budget is to track your income and expenses. Start by gathering all your financial statements, including bank statements, credit card bills, and receipts. Categorize your expenses into different categories, such as housing, transportation, food, entertainment, and savings. This will give you a clear picture of where your money is going and help identify areas where you can cut back or make adjustments.

Next, set financial goals for yourself. Whether you aim to save for a down payment on a house, invest in stocks and shares, or pay off debt, having clear goals will help you stay motivated and focused. Break down your goals into short-term, medium-term, and long-term objectives, and assign a realistic timeline and monetary value to each.

Once you have identified your goals, it's time to create a budget that aligns with your financial objectives. Start by allocating a portion of your income towards essential expenses such as rent, utilities, and groceries. Then, determine how much you can comfortably save and invest each month. It is necessary to prioritize savings and investments to ensure long-term financial security and growth.

Remember to leave room for discretionary spending and entertainment. Allocating a small portion of your budget for leisure activities will help you maintain a healthy work-life balance while staying on track toward your financial goals.

To ensure the success of your budget, it is crucial to review and adjust it periodically. As your income and expenses fluctuate, make necessary amendments to your budget to reflect these changes accurately. Regularly monitoring your budget will help you stay accountable and make informed financial decisions.

Creating a personal budget is a fundamental step toward achieving financial freedom. By tracking your income and expenses, setting clear goals, and allocating your resources wisely, you can effectively manage your finances and make informed decisions regarding stocks and shares. Remember, discipline and consistency are essential to financial success, so stay committed to your budget and adjust it as necessary to achieve your long-term financial goals.

Debt Management and Reduction

This subchapter will delve into the crucial topic of debt management and reduction. Debt can significantly burden individuals and families, hindering their financial well-being and preventing them from achieving their goals. By understanding the principles of debt management and implementing effective strategies, you can take control of your financial situation and pave the way toward a debt-free future.

Understanding Debt:

Debt is an obligation owed by an individual or entity to another party. It can come in various forms, such as credit card debt, student loans, mortgages, or personal loans. While debt can sometimes be necessary, like when purchasing a home or investing in education, it is essential to manage it wisely to avoid unnecessary financial stress and long-term consequences.

Creating a Debt Management Plan:

Creating a comprehensive plan is the first step towards debt management and reduction. Start by assessing your current financial situation, including income, expenses, and outstanding debts. Identify each debt's interest rates, minimum payments, and due dates. This will help you prioritize which debts to tackle first.

Strategies for Debt Reduction:

There are several effective strategies for reducing debt, and choosing the one that suits your financial circumstances best is essential. Two popular methods are the debt snowball and debt avalanche. The debt snowball approach involves paying off the smallest debt first while making minimum payments on other debts. Once the smallest debt is paid off, the freed-up funds are redirected toward the next smallest debt until all obligations are eliminated. On the other hand, the debt avalanche method focuses on paying off debts with the highest interest rates first, saving you money on interest payments over time.

Additional Tips for Debt Management:

In addition to the strategies above, there are other steps you can take to manage and reduce your debt effectively. These include negotiating lower interest rates with creditors, consolidating multiple debts into a single loan with a lower interest rate, and seeking professional advice from credit counselling agencies.

Conclusion:

Debt management and reduction is a vital aspect of achieving financial freedom. By understanding the principles of debt management and implementing effective strategies, you can take control of your financial situation and work towards a debt-free future. Remember, it's never too late to start managing your debt and making choices that will positively impact your economic well-being. With discipline, perseverance, and a solid plan, you can conquer your debts and pave the way for a brighter financial future.

Saving and Investing for Retirement

Saving and investing for retirement is crucial to ensuring financial security and freedom in the later stages of life. In this subchapter, we will explore the various strategies and options available for individuals to secure a comfortable retirement through saving and investing in stocks and shares.

Retirement planning requires a proactive approach, as relying solely on pension plans or government programs may not be sufficient to meet one's financial needs during retirement. Therefore, it is essential to start saving early and consistently, even if the amounts seem small initially. Compound interest can work wonders over time, allowing investments to grow exponentially.

One of the most effective ways to save for retirement is through employer-sponsored retirement plans, such as 401(k) or 403(b) plans. These plans offer tax advantages and often include employer-matching contributions, which can significantly boost your savings. Contributing the maximum amount the program allows to take full advantage of these benefits is wise.

Individual Retirement Accounts (IRAs) are another popular option for retirement savings. Traditional IRAs offer tax-deferred growth, meaning you won't pay taxes on the contributions or earnings until you withdraw the funds during retirement. Roth IRAs, on the other hand, provide tax-free growth, allowing you to remove the funds tax-free in retirement. These accounts offer flexibility and control over your investments.

When investing for retirement, stocks and shares can play a vital role in building wealth over the long term. While they carry a higher risk level than other investment options, stocks and shares have historically provided higher returns. Diversifying your portfolio by investing in a mix of stocks, bonds, and other assets can help mitigate risk and ensure the steady growth of your investments.

Investing in index or exchange-traded funds (ETFs) is a popular strategy for retirement investors. These funds track a specific market index, providing instant diversification and low expense ratios. They are ideal for passive investors who want to minimize the time and effort required to manage their portfolios.

For those with a higher risk tolerance, investing in individual stocks can offer the potential for higher returns. However, thorough research and analysis are crucial to make informed investment decisions. It is advisable to seek guidance from a financial advisor or educate oneself on stock analysis techniques to increase the chances of success.

In conclusion, saving and investing for retirement is a lifelong process that requires discipline, planning, and knowledge. By starting early, taking advantage of tax-advantaged retirement accounts, and diversifying investments in stocks and shares, individuals can build a solid financial foundation for a comfortable retirement. It is never too late to start; the sooner one takes action, the better off they will be.

Long-Term Wealth-Building Strategies

In this subchapter of "Financial Freedom: A Beginner's Guide to Stocks and Shares, " we will delve into the essential long-term wealth-building strategies to help you achieve financial independence and secure your future. Whether you are a beginner or have some knowledge of finance, stocks, and shares, these strategies will guide you on your path to success.

1. Diversification: The first key strategy is diversifying your investment portfolio. You can mitigate risks and maximise potential returns by spreading your investments across different asset classes, industries, and geographical locations. Diversification helps protect your wealth from market fluctuations and ensures you are not overly dependent on a single investment.

2. Dollar-Cost Averaging: Another effective strategy is dollar-cost averaging. This approach involves regularly investing a fixed amount of money, regardless of market conditions. By consistently investing over time, you can take advantage of market fluctuations, buying more shares when prices are low and fewer when prices are high. This method helps smooth out the impact of short-term market volatility and allows you to benefit from the long-term growth potential of your investments.

3. Compound Interest: Compound interest is one of the most powerful wealth-building tools. You can earn interest on your initial and accumulated investments by reinvesting

your earnings. Over time, this compounding effect can significantly boost your returns and accelerate your wealth accumulation. Starting early and staying consistent with your investments gives compound interest ample time to work magic.

4. Active vs. Passive Investing: When building long-term wealth, it is essential to understand the difference between active and passive investing. Active investing involves researching and selecting individual stocks to outperform the market. Passive investing, on the other hand, consists of investing in index funds or exchange-traded funds (ETFs) that track the performance of a specific market index. Both approaches have their merits, and finding the right balance can help you achieve your financial goals.

5. Patience and Discipline: Long-term wealth building requires patience and discipline. It is crucial to resist making impulsive decisions based on short-term market fluctuations. Stay focused on your long-term investment objectives, regularly review and rebalance your portfolio, and avoid emotional reactions to market volatility.

By following these long-term wealth-building strategies, you can harness the power of the stock market and shares to secure a financially independent future. Remember, financial freedom is a journey, and starting early with a solid plan will set you on the path to success.

Chapter 9

Tax Considerations for Stock Market Investors

Understanding Capital Gains Tax

When investing in stocks and shares, it is crucial to have a comprehensive understanding of the various taxes that may impact your investment returns. One such tax that investors must be aware of is capital gains tax (CGT). This subchapter will delve into the critical aspects of capital gains tax and how it affects your financial freedom.

Capital gains tax is imposed on the profit from selling certain assets, including stocks and shares. It is important to note that CGT only applies when you sell an asset and realize a gain. The tax is not levied on the unrealized gains or the value of your investments in the market.

The capital gains tax rate varies depending on your income level and the asset's holding period. In general, short-term capital gains are taxed more than long-term gains. Short-term gains refer to profits made on investments held for less than a year, while long-term gains are made for more than a year.

Determining your taxable gain to calculate your capital gains tax liability would be best. This can be done by subtracting the cost basis (the initial purchase price) from the asset's selling price. However, it is essential to note that certain adjustments and deductions may apply in specific circumstances, such as including transaction costs or capital losses.

Some certain exemptions and allowances can help reduce your capital gains tax liability. For instance, many countries offer a tax-free allowance up to a certain threshold. Additionally, investments held within tax-advantaged accounts like Individual Retirement Accounts (IRAs) or 401(k)s may be subject to different tax rules.

Understanding the intricacies of capital gains tax is essential for investors to make informed decisions and optimize their investment strategies. By considering the tax implications of buying and selling stocks and shares, you can effectively manage your tax liability and maximize your overall returns.

In conclusion, capital gains tax is a crucial consideration for investors in stocks and shares. By understanding how this tax works, the applicable rates, and the available exemptions, investors can navigate the tax landscape more effectively and achieve financial freedom. It is crucial to consult with a tax professional or financial advisor to ensure compliance with tax regulations and to develop a tax-efficient investment plan.

Tax-Advantaged Investment Accounts

Understanding the tax implications can significantly impact your overall returns when investing in stocks and shares. Fortunately, there are tax-advantaged investment accounts that can help you optimize your investments and minimize your tax burden. This subchapter will explore the different types of tax-advantaged investment accounts available to individuals, providing an overview of their benefits.

One popular tax-advantaged investment account is the Individual Retirement Account (IRA). IRAs come in two main types: Traditional IRA and Roth IRA. The Traditional IRA allows you to contribute pre-tax dollars, reducing your taxable income for the year of contribution. However, withdrawals from a Traditional IRA are subject to income tax. On the other hand, Roth IRAs are funded with after-tax dollars, meaning your contributions are not tax-deductible. However, the growth and withdrawals from a Roth IRA are tax-free, making it an attractive option for long-term investors.

Another tax-advantaged investment account is the 401(k), which employers typically offer. Like a Traditional IRA, 401(k) contributions are made with pre-tax dollars, reducing your taxable income. Employers often match a percentage of your donations, making it a valuable investment tool. However, 401(k) withdrawals are subject to income tax. It's important to note that IRAs and 401(k)s have contribution limits and specific withdrawal rules, so it's crucial to consult a financial advisor or tax professional to understand the nuances.

In addition to IRAs and 401(k)s, there are other tax-advantaged investment accounts, such as Health Savings Accounts (HSAs) and Education Savings Accounts (ESAs). HSAs help individuals save for medical expenses, offering tax deductions on contributions, tax-free growth, and tax-free withdrawals for qualified medical expenses. ESAs, on the other hand, are specifically for educational expenses, providing tax-free growth and tax-free withdrawals for qualified education expenses.

By utilizing tax-advantaged investment accounts, you can maximize your investment potential while minimizing your tax liability. These accounts offer a range of benefits, from tax deductions to tax-free growth and withdrawals, depending on the specific account type. However, it's essential to consider your financial goals and circumstances before choosing the most suitable tax-advantaged investment account. Remember, consulting with a financial advisor or tax professional can provide valuable insights and help you make informed decisions aligning with your financial strategy.

Tax-Efficient Investing Strategies

When it comes to investing in stocks and shares, one aspect that is often overlooked is the tax implications. Taxes can eat into your investment returns, reducing the overall profitability of your portfolio. However, with careful planning and knowledge of tax-efficient investing strategies, you can minimize your tax burden and maximize your investment gains. This subchapter will explore critical techniques to help you achieve financial freedom while optimizing your tax situation.

1. Utilize tax-advantaged accounts: One of the most effective ways to minimize taxes on your investments is to take advantage of tax-advantaged accounts such as Individual Retirement Accounts (IRAs), 401(k)s, or similar retirement plans. These accounts offer tax benefits, such as tax-deductible contributions or tax-free growth, allowing your investments to grow without being subject to immediate taxes.

2. Consider tax-efficient investment vehicles: Certain investment vehicles, such as index funds or exchange-traded funds (ETFs), are known for their tax efficiency.

These funds typically have low turnover rates, generating fewer taxable events. By investing in these vehicles, you can reduce the taxes you owe, as capital gains distributions are minimized.

3. Tax-loss harvesting: This strategy involves selling investments that have experienced losses to offset capital gains in your portfolio. By strategically harvesting these losses, you can reduce your taxable income, potentially lowering your overall tax liability. However, it is essential to be mindful of the wash-sale rule, which restricts repurchasing a substantially identical security within 30 days to claim the tax loss.

4. Asset location: Another tax-efficient strategy is to place investments in the most tax-efficient accounts. Generally, investments that generate higher income levels, such as bonds or real estate investment trusts (REITs), are better suited for tax-advantaged accounts. In contrast, lower-income investments, such as stocks, can be held in taxable accounts. This way, you can minimize the taxes paid on interest, dividends, and capital gains.

5. Long-term investing: Holding investments for the long term can also have tax advantages. Investments held for over a year qualify for long-term capital gains tax rates, typically lower than short-term rates. By adopting a long-term investment strategy, you can benefit from the preferential tax treatment associated with long-term gains.

It is crucial to consult with a qualified tax professional or financial advisor to assess your specific tax situation and determine the most suitable tax-efficient strategies for your investment goals. By implementing these strategies, you can optimize your investment returns while keeping your tax bill under control, ultimately inching closer to financial freedom.

Reporting Stock Market Gains and Losses

When investing in the stock market, understanding how to report gains and losses is crucial. As an investor, keeping track of your financial performance accurately and efficiently is essential. This subchapter will guide you through writing stock market gains and losses, providing you with the knowledge and tools to monitor and evaluate your investments effectively.

Reporting gains and losses in the stock market involves calculating and documenting the difference between your shares' purchase and sale prices. This calculation determines your profit or loss on each transaction. It is important to note that gains and losses are not realized until the shares are sold. Until then, they are considered unrealized gains or losses and may fluctuate with market conditions.

To report your gains and losses, you must keep a detailed record of your transactions, including the date of purchase, the number of shares, the purchase price, the date of sale, the selling price, and any associated fees or commissions. This information will be helpful when preparing your tax returns or assessing your overall investment performance.

There are various methods for reporting gains and losses, such as FIFO (First In, First Out) and specific identification. FIFO assumes that the first shares purchased are the first ones sold, while clear identification allows you to choose which shares to trade based on their cost basis. It is essential to consult with a tax professional or financial advisor to determine the most suitable method for your situation.

In addition to reporting gains and losses for tax purposes, it is equally important to analyze your investment performance regularly. This will help you identify trends, evaluate the success of your investment strategy, and make informed decisions for future investments. Many financial platforms offer tools and reports to assist you in tracking your portfolio's performance, including overall gains and losses.

By understanding how to report gains and losses in the stock market, you are taking a significant step toward achieving financial freedom. Consistently monitoring and evaluating your investments will allow you to make informed decisions and maximize your returns. Remember to consult with professionals and utilize available resources to ensure accurate reporting and analysis of your stock market gains and losses.

Seeking Professional Tax Advice

Understanding the tax implications is crucial when managing your finances and investing in stocks and shares. The ever-changing tax laws and regulations can be complex and overwhelming for the average investor. That's why it is highly recommended to seek professional tax advice to ensure you are making informed decisions and maximizing your returns.

Tax planning is an essential component of any successful investment strategy. A professional tax advisor can provide valuable insights and guidance on minimising your tax liabilities while maximizing your investment gains. They can help you navigate the intricacies of tax laws, identify potential tax-saving opportunities, and ensure you comply with all necessary tax obligations.

One of the primary benefits of seeking professional tax advice is optimising your investment portfolio. By understanding the tax implications of different investment vehicles, such as stocks, bonds, or mutual funds, you can make informed decisions that align with your financial goals. A tax advisor can assist you in structuring your investments tax-efficiently, taking advantage of deductions, exemptions, and credits that may be available to you.

Furthermore, a tax professional can guide you through tax filing, ensuring accuracy and minimizing the risk of costly errors. They can help you gather and organize all the necessary financial documents, such as investment statements, dividend reports, and capital gains records. By entrusting your tax filings to a professional, you can have peace of mind knowing that someone with expertise in the field is handling your taxes.

Additionally, a tax advisor can keep you updated on any changes to tax laws that may impact your investments. They can provide ongoing advice and recommend adjustments to your investment strategy to optimize tax efficiency. By staying informed and proactive, you can save significant money in taxes over the long term.

In conclusion, seeking professional tax advice is essential for anyone interested in investing in stocks and shares. The expertise and guidance provided by a tax advisor can help you navigate the complexities of tax laws, optimize your investment portfolio, and minimize your tax liabilities. By making informed decisions and staying ahead of tax changes, you can achieve financial freedom and maximize your returns in the world of stocks and shares.

Chapter 10

Common Mistakes to Avoid in Stock Market Investing

Chasing Hot Stocks and Market Trends

In the fast-paced world of finance, it's easy to get caught up in the allure of chasing hot stocks and market trends. The promise of quick profits and overnight success can be enticing, especially for beginner investors looking to make their mark in the world of stocks and shares. However, it is essential to approach this strategy with caution and a clear understanding of its potential risks.

Hot stocks refer to companies experiencing rapid growth or have recently made headlines for some reason. These stocks often generate a buzz and attract a lot of attention from investors. While it is true that investing in these stocks can yield significant returns, it is crucial to remember that such success stories are the exception rather than the norm.

One of the main pitfalls of chasing hot stocks is the difficulty in accurately predicting which ones will continue to perform well in the long term. The stock market is inherently unpredictable, and trends can change rapidly. It's crucial to conduct thorough research and analysis before investing in any hot stock, considering factors such as the company's financial health, industry trends, and competitive landscape.

On the other hand, market trends involve identifying patterns or movements in the market as a whole. Various factors, including economic indicators, political events, and global developments, can influence these trends. While staying informed about market trends is essential, unthinkingly following them without a solid investment strategy can be dangerous.

One common mistake novice investors make is buying stocks at the peak of a trend when prices are inflated. This can lead to buying high and selling low, resulting in substantial losses. It is important to remember that trends are not guaranteed to continue indefinitely, and it's crucial to exercise caution and make informed decisions based on a comprehensive understanding of the market.

Instead of chasing hot stocks and market trends, a more prudent approach to investing in stocks and shares is to focus on long-term value and diversification. By investing in a diversified portfolio of well-established companies with solid fundamentals, investors can mitigate risk and build wealth over time.

In conclusion, chasing hot stocks and market trends can be tempting, but it is not a foolproof strategy. While staying informed and aware of market movements is essential, conducting thorough research and making informed decisions is equally crucial. Investors can increase their chances of achieving financial freedom in stocks and shares by focusing on long-term value and diversification.

Overtrading and Frequent Buying/Selling

Buying and selling to maximise profits can be tempting in the fast-paced world of stocks and shares. However, this approach, known as overtrading, can often lead to poor investment decisions and ultimately hinder your financial freedom. This subchapteThisill explore the dangers of overtrading and frequent buying/selling, providing valuable insights to help you navigate the complexities of the finance stocks and shares market.

Overtrading occurs when investors excessively buy and sell, driven by emotions rather than rational analysis. The allure of quick profits and the fear of missing out can cloud judgment, leading to impulsive decisions that may result in financial losses. It is crucial to understand that investing is a long-term game, and success lies in building a well-diversified portfolio based on solid research and analysis.

Frequent buying/selling is closely linked to overtrading, which involves making numerous trades quickly. While it may seem like an active and involved approach, it can often lead to high transaction costs and increased taxes, eating into your overall returns. Moreover, constant trading can prevent you from reaping the benefits of compounding, one of the most powerful wealth-building tools in the stock market.

To avoid falling, It is essential to develop a disciplined investment strategy to avoid the trap of overtrading and frequent buying/selling; it is necessary to have clear and realistic financial goals, whether saving for retirement, funding your child's education, or achieving a specific financial milestone. With a defined purpose, you can resist the urge to make impulsive trades and focus on long-term growth.

Additionally, conducting thorough research and analysis before making investment decisions is crucial. Take the time to understand the company's fundamentals, evaluate its growth potential, and assess its competitive position in the market. By adopting a thoughtful and informed approach, you can make sound investment choices that align with your financial goals.

Furthermore, having a well-diversified portfolio plays a significant role in mitigating the risks associated with overtrading. Spread your investments across different sectors, industries, and asset classes to ensure that a single loss does not significantly impact your overall portfolio. Regularly reviewing and rebalancing your holdings can help maintain a healthy mix of investments and prevent unnecessary buying/selling activities.

In conclusion, overtrading and frequent buying/selling can hinder your financial freedom in stocks and shares. By understanding the dangers associated with these practices and adopting a disciplined investment strategy, you can pave the way toward long-term success. Remember, investing is not a race but a journey that requires patience, knowledge, and strategic decision-making.

Neglecting Research and Due Diligence

In the fast-paced world of finance, it is easy to get caught up in the excitement and rush of investing in stocks and shares. However, one crucial mistake beginners often make is neglecting to conduct proper research and due diligence before making investment decisions. This subchapter sheds light on the importance of thorough analysis and due diligence and how it can pave the way for financial freedom in the stock market.

Research is the foundation of successful investing. It involves gathering and analyzing information about companies, industries, and market trends to make informed decisions. Without research, investors are gambling with their hard-earned money, as they lack the necessary knowledge to make sound investment choices. By neglecting research, investors expose themselves to unnecessary risks and increase the likelihood of losses.

Due diligence is conducting a comprehensive investigation into a potential investment opportunity. It goes beyond basic research and involves assessing the financial heaa company, management team, competitive position, and company growth prospects. Nediligence can lead to investing in companies with weak fundamentals or questionable practices, which can have disastrous consequences for one's financial portfolio.

Understanding the importance of research and due diligence is vital for those interested in finance, stocks, and shared niches, undsharedding te. Understanding formed decimals based on facts rather than emotions or rumours. By dedicating the necessary time and effort to research, investors can identify undervalued companies, uncover emerging trends, and spot potential risks before they become significant problems.

Moreover, research and due diligence allow investors to develop a long-term investment strategy and stay focused on their financial goals. It helps them build a diversified portfolio, mitigating potential risks and maximizing potential returns. By investing in companies they understand and have thoroughly researched, investors can have confidence in their choices, even during market downturns.

In conclusion, neglecting research and due diligence is a grave mistake that can hinder financial freedom in stocks and shares; by emphasizing this, it equips general readers and finance, stocks, and shares enthusiasts with the knowledge and tools necessary to make informed investment decisions. Remember, success by emphasising the importance of research and due diligence in the stock market is not solely based on luck but rather on the abolition of research, analysis, and due diligence.

Failing to Diversify Properly

One of the most crucial concepts to understand when investing in stocks and shares is diversification. Unfortunately, many investors, even experienced ones, fail to diversify correctly, often leading to significant financial losses. In this subchapter, we will delve into the importance of diversification and the potential consequences of neglecting this fundamental principle.

Diversification is the practice of spreading your investments across a range of different assets, industries, and geographic regions. The goal is to minimize risk by avoiding overexposure to any single investment. By diversifying your portfolio, you can potentially protect yourself from the volatility of individual stocks, shares, and economies that may affect specific sectors or regions.

One common mistake investors make is putting all their eggs in one basket. This is often driven by a lack of knowledge or a misguided belief that they have discovered a surefire investment opportunity. However, even the most promising stocks and shares can experience unexpected setbacks, causing significant losses for those who fail to diversify.

Another pitfall investors often fall into is focusing solely on a specific niche or industry. While it is crucial to have a ding of the sectors you invest in, relying on to hea is crucially on a single industry can leave your portfolio vulnerable to sector-specific risks. For example, if you have heavily invested in technology stocks and the tech sector experiences a downturn, your entire investment may suffer.

Furthermore, diversification should not be limited to a single country or geographic region. Economic conditions and geopolitical events can significantly impact the performance of specific markets. By spreading your investments across different nations, you can reduce the risk associated with a single market and take advantage of potential opportunities in emerging economies.

In conclusion, failing to diversify correctly is a grave mistake that can have significant financial consequences. It is crucial for both beginners and experienced investors to understand the importance of diversification and to implement it effectively in their investment strategies. By spreading your investments across various assets, industries, and geographic regions, you can protect yourself from unforeseen risks and increase your chances of achieving financial freedom in stocks and shares.

Letting Emotions Drive Investment Decisions

In the fast-paced world of finance, making sound investment decisions is crucial for achieving financial freedom. However, many individuals succumb to a common pitfall: allowing emotions to drive their investment choices. In this subchapter, we will explore the detrimental effects of emotional decision-making and provide strategies to help you make rational investment choices.

Emotions like fear and like can cloud judgment and lead to poor investment outcomes. When the market is booming, greed may push you to invest heavily without considering the potential risks. On the other hand, fear can cause panic selling during market downturns, leading to missed opportunities for long-term growth. Recognising and controlling these emotions in essential decisions can harm your financial goals.

Developing a well-defined investment plan to counter emotional decision-making is to create and adopt a long-term perspective; you can avoid making impulsive decisions based on short-term market fluctuations. Please stick to your goal, even when emotions tempt you to deviate. Remember, successful investing is a marathon, not a sprint.

Another valuable technique is conducting a thorough analysis before making investment decisions. Understand the fundamentals of the companies or assets you are considering and evaluate their growth potential. By focusing on yourself, you can make more informed choices with objective information rather than emotional impulses and make your investment portfolio crucial. Spreading your investments across different asset classes and sectors can help mitigate risk and reduce the impact of emotional decision-making. When one investment underperforms, others may compensate, minimizing potential losses.

Seeking advice from professionals in the finance industry can also be beneficial. Financial advisors or wealth managers can provide objective guidance and help you stay on track with your investment plan. They have experience managing emotions and can offer valuable insights during turbulent market conditions.

Lastly, cultivating a disciplined mindset is essential. Embrace rationality and avoid being swayed by short-term market sentiment. Remember your long-term financial goals and that successful investing requires time and perseverance.

In conclusion, emotions can be detrimental to investment decisions. By developing a wYou can overcome emotional biases and make rational choices by defining a plan, conducting thorough research, diversifying your portfolio, seeking professional advice, and fostering a disciplined mindset; you can overcome financial freedom through stocks and shares, which requires a balanced approach prioritising long-term growth over short-term.

Chapter 11

<hr>

Developing a Winning Mindset for Stock Market Success

Patience and Discipline

In the fast-paced world of finance, patience and discipline are two essential virtues that can significantly impact your success in the stock market. A beginner's guide to stocks and shares would be incomplete without emphasizing the importance of these qualities to achieve financial freedom.

Patience plays a crucial role in navigating the ups and downs of the stock market. It is natural for investors to seek quick returns and get tempted by the allure of overnight success. However, it is essential to remember that investing is a long-term game. Stocks and shares may experience short-term fluctuations, but it is the patient and the patient investors.

By adopting a patAdoptingch, you give your i gives time to grow and ride out market volatility. This allows you to make well-informed decisions rather than being swayed by short-term market trends. Patience also helps you avoid impulsive buying or selling, often leading to costly mistakes. Remember, Rome wasn't built in a day, and neither is a solid investment portfolio.

Discipline goes hand in hand with patience when achieving financial freedom through stocks and shares. It involves sticking to a well-defined investment plan and avoiding emotional decision-making. Discipline helps you focus on your long-term goals, even in market turbulence.

Developing a disciplined approach requires setting clear investment objectives, determining risk tolerance, and establishing a diversified portfolio. Regularly reviewing and rebalancing your investments is crucial to ensure they align with your financial goals. Discipline prevents you from chasing the latest hot stock or making impulsive trades based on fear or greed.

It is worth noting that patience and discipline are not innate qualities but can be cultivated through knowledge and practice. Educating yourself about the fundamentals of finance, stocks, and shares is a vital first step. Understanding Understandingorks and analyzing financial statements allows you to make decisions based on sound reasoning rather than relying on luck or speculation.

In conclusion, patience and discipline are the pillars of success in stocks and shares. They empower you to make rational decisions, stay focused on your long-term goals, and weather the storms of market volatility. By incorporating these virtues into your investment strategy, you are well on your way to achieving financial freedom.

Learning from Mistakes

Mistakes are an inherent part of life, and the world of finance is no exception. Making mistakes is often seen as essential to freedom. In this subchapter, we will explore the valuable lessons that can be learned from our mistakes when investing in stocks and shares.

One of the most significant mistakes beginners make is jumping into the stock market without proper research or understanding. It is crucial to take the time to educate yourself about the basics of finance, stocks, and shares before diving headfirst into the market. By doing so, you can avoid making rash decisions based on emotions or hearsay.

Another common mistake is failing to diversify your investment portfolio. Placing all your eggs in one basket can be extremely risky. Instead, spreading across different sectors, industries, and geographical locations is advisable. Diversification is advisable to help minimize the impact of potential losses and increase your chances of making profitable investments.

Timing the market is yet another mistake many investors make. Trying to predict short-term fluctuations in stock prices is an incredibly challenging task, even for seasoned professionals. Instead, focus on the long-term proa company's or industry's long-term prospects investment decisions. Remember, investing is a marathon, not a sprint.

It is also essential to learn from past mistakes. Keeping a record of your investments, including successes and failures, can help you identify patterns and avoid repeating the same errors. Reflect on what went wrong, analyze your decisions, and use these lessons to refine your investment strategy going forward.

Additionally, adjusting according to your financial goals and stage in life is crucial. As a beginner, it is prudent to start with safer investments and gradually increase your risk appetite as you gain more experience and knowledge.

Lastly, seek guidance from experienced investors or financial advisors who can provide valuable insights and help you navigate the complex world of stocks and shares. Learning from the mistakes of others can save you from potentially costly errors and accelerate your path toward financial freedom.

In conclusion, mistakes are an inevitable part of the learning process, a part Finland shares. Finland's shared common pitfalls, and by learning from our missteps, we can refine our investment strategies, minimize risks, and increase our chances of achieving long-term financial success.

Staying Informed and Educated

In the fast-paced world of finance, it is crucial to stay informed and educated to achieve financial freedom through stocks and shares. This subchapter will explore strategies and resources to help general re and niche enthusiasts find shares, enhance their knowledge, and make informed investment decisions.

1. Reading Financial News: Staying updated with the latest happenings in the financial world is essential. General readers can start by subscribing to reputable financial newspapers or magazines that provide daily or weekly updates on market trends, economic indicators, and company news. Niche enthusiasts can consider specialized publications that delve deeper into stock market analysis, investment strategies, and expert opinions.

2. Online Resources: With the advent of the internet, a wealth of information is available at our fingertips. General readers can explore financial websites and blogs that offer beginner-friendly guides, tutorials, and market news. For niche enthusiasts, platforvesting forums, online communities,

and educational websites provide analysis, stock recommendations, and interactive learning opportunities.

3. Financial Podcasts and Webinars: For those who prefer audio or visual content, podcasts and webinars can be a great way to stay informed. General readers can listen to beginner-friendly financial podcasts that cover a wide range of topics, including stocks and shares. Niche enthusiasts can opt for webinars conducted by industry experts, where they can use advanced investment strategies and market analysis.

4. Investment Courses and Seminars: To better understand stocks and shares, general readers and niche enthusiasts can consider enrolling in investment courses or attending seminars. These educational programs provide structured learning, covering various aspects of finance, including stock market fundamentals, technical analysis, and risk management. Investing in education can significantly enhance one's ability to make informed investment decisions.

5. Social Media and Networking: Engaging with like-minded individuals on social media platforms can be an excellent way to learn

from others and expand one's knowledge base. General readers can follow reputable finance influencers and participate in discussions to gain insights into the stock market. Niche enthusiasts can join specialized finance groups or forums to network with professionals and gain access to valuable resources.

Staying informed and educated is an ongoing process in the ever-evolving world of stocks and shares. By incorporating these strategies and utilizing the available resources, both general readers and niche enthusiasts can enhance their financial knowledge, make informed investment decisions, and work towards achieving their financial freedom.

Setting Realistic Goals and Expectations

In the pursuit of financial freedom, it is crucial to set realistic goals and expectations. This subchapter aims to guide general readers and those interested in finance shares on establishing achievable targets and maintaining rational expectations.

Regarding investors and shares, it is essential to begin by setting clear and attainable goals. These goals should be specific, measurable, achievable, relevant, and time-bound (SMART). For instance, instead of developing a vague objective like "making a lot of money, " a more specific goal could be "earning a 10% return on investment within two years. " Setting such specific targets helps to stay focused and motivated throughout the investment journey.

Furthermore, it is crucial to align your risk tolerance and financial situation. Assessing your risk tolerance is essential and will help you determine the type of investments that suit you best. If you have a low-risk tolerance, investing in stable blue-chip stocks may be more. To invest in have a higher risk tolerance, you might consider investing in more volatile growth stocks. Additionally, evaluating your financial situation, including your income, expenses, and debt, will give you a better understanding of how much capital you can comfortably allocate towards investing.

While setting goals is essential, it is equally vital to maintain realistic expectations. The stock market can be unpredictable, and it is necessary to acknowledge that investments carry inherent risks. Understanding that the market can fluctuate and that losses are possible will help you maintain a realistic perspective. It is essential to avoid getting caught up in the hype and not to expect extraordinary returns overnight.

Conducting thorough research and knowledge of the stock market helps foster realistic expectations. Educating yourself is beneficial to learn about various investment strategies, market trends, and company fundamentals and will enable you to make informed decisions and manage your expectations accordingly.

Lastly, reviewing and reassessing your goals and expectations is essential. The stock market is dynamic, and your financial situation may change over time. By periodically evaluating and adjusting your objectives, you can ensure they remain ant and attainable, given the current circumstances.

In conclusion, setting realistic goals and expectations is paramount for anyone venturing into the world of stocks and shares. By establishing specific and attainable objectives, aligning them with your risk tolerance and financial situation, and maintaining a realistic perspective, you are setting yourself up for a more prosperous and fulfilling investment journey toward financial freedom.

Cultivating a Long-Term Perspective

In the fast-paced world of finance, it is easy to get caught up in short-term fluctuations and trends. However, if you want financial freedom, cultivate a long-term perspective when investing in stocks and shares. This subchapter will delve into the importance of adopting this mindset and provide practical tips to help you navigate the ever-changing landscape of the stock market.

Why is a long-term perspective critical? The stock market is notorious for its volatility, with prices fluctuating daily. It is easy to get swayed by these short-term movements and make impulsive decisions that can negatively impact your portfolio. By adopting a long-term perspective, you can ride out these short-term fluctuations and focus on the bigger picture – the potential for long-term growth and wealth creation.

One of the key benefits of a long-term perspective is the power of compounding. Investing in investing with a long-term horizon gives you time to grow and benefit from compounding returns. Compounding is the process by which gains generate additional gains over time. The longer you stay invested, the greater the potential for compounding to work magic and exponentially grow your wealth.

To cultivate a long-term perspective, developing an investment plan is essential. This plan is vital to outline your financial goals, risk tolerance, and investment time horizon. With a clearWith, you can avoid knee-jerk reactions to market fluctuations and stay focused on your long-term objectives. Regularly reviewing and adjusting your plan is also crucial, as your financial circumstances and goals may change over time.

Another aspect of cultivating a long-term perspective is practising patience and practising discipline. Chasing hot stock or engaging in frequent trading can be tempting. It has shown that systematic often leads to lower and transactions adopting buy-and-hold and the to tinker your from long-term of investments. conclusion, cultivating long-term is for financial through and allows to short-term fluctuations, benefit the of stay on long-term developing well-defined plan practisingPatient exercising. Discipline, you set up long-term in fina12: and Steps. Key subchapteThisill critical discussed the "Financial A Guide Stocks Shares. Whether are general or a interest finance, stocks, and these concepts essential financial

1. Stocks Shares: the of book, we the of and represent in company, while refer the units stock. Investing stocks shares provide for wealth

2. Risk Return: of most concepts finance the between and returns come higher crucial evaluate goals diving the market. is Diversifying investment is for risk. By your across asset and can yourself losses the Analysis: the aspects a as financial advantage, and prospects, is for informed decisions. This involves financial trends, and factors. Analysis: analysis studying price volume to future movements. It analyzing indicators short-term decisions. Indexes: indexes, such the 500 Dow Industrial a of that as for overall performance. Monitoring indexes investors the health compare performance. Management: risk involves realistic your implementing orders limit losses. It's to various management to your

8. Investing Various strategies, such value investing, or investing, can you your goals. Each has own of considerations. reviewing key gain solid in and you confidently informed and the markets—ssSuccessfules learning, adaptation, and updated

Taking and Started

In fast-paced freedom a many to those the step, it be for stocks shares; the aims provide guide help take and started your freedom. diving the of is to the and represent in company, and in allows to a ownership you benefit the profits growth. However, it essential note investing stocks shares carries it crucial be of before any

The step taking is educate are resources books, online financial can you a understanding how stock works. By yourself knowledge, you be equipped make decisions navigate complexities the

Once have excellent of fundamentals, we a plan. Determine investment short-term long-term, and a for is to with small and increase investment you experience confidence. a firm another step getting for reputable that user-friendly fees, and wide of options. Take time research firms compare services find one best your

Now you a and brokerage is to investing. Begin diversifying portfolio, which investing various and across industries. This helps risks increases chances success. Remember investing a commitment, and is to disciplined avoid impulsive based short-term fluctuations. monitor investments stay with trends. Review portfolio and necessary based your and conditions. Remember, investing a learning it essential stay and your accordingly. action getting on journey financial may overwhelming, but the knowledge, planning, and is achievable following steps in subchapter, you be on way building successful portfolio securing financial

Seeking Education Resources

In fast-paced of ahead the is you a investor just further and is to financial in stock subchapter to you valuable on to your and to informed decisions. plays vital in journey financial equips with necessary and to the world stocks shares. There various to your knowledge. One the popular is in or workshops by financial or programs traditional and analysis, risk   strategic planning. Additionally, online and websites convenient to reading tutorials, and

Another   resource   joining   forums communities to   shares. These allow to with individuals, share learn experts the in and questions provide insights perspectives may your knowledge help refine investment

Financial outlets, such Bloomberg, CNBC, and Times, offer regarding latest trends, company economic informed global news help make investment and potential or

Furthermore, developing written renowned and experts crucial. These provide insights successful strategies, market   the of professionals. Some titles "The Investor" Benjamin Random Down Street" Burton "Common and Profits" Philip

Remember, seeking education resources an process. The world dynamic, and with latest investment is   continuously your base leveraging resources, you enhance chances achieving freedom the world stocks shares. with Market today's world, engaging stock communities essential building knowledge finding in and you're beginner an investor, participating these can valuable for a environment learn others. of first to with market is where communities forums, social groups, and websites great to platforms individuals a interest finance, stocks, and them spaces connect like-minded

Once found right essential actively in discussions lights, ask seek from members. Engaging these allows to from experiences, helps connections, and your within finance

Remember, engaging stock is just asking advice; also giving your guidance beginners, and to overall environment. By an participant, you yourself a community from

Furthermore, attending market conferences another way engage the and your gatherings opportunities meet experts, learn the trends, and relationships fellow sure take to your of stock and with individuals the

Lastly, it's to stock communities a mindset. While communities valuable and what receive crucial. Remember it essential the market dynamic complex, and may the to different and informed based your

Engaging stock communities a tool anyone in shares. By participating, giving receiving events, and discussions a mindset, you harness power these to your knowledge, develop investment ultimately financial

Embracing Journey Financial today's world, attaining freedom like elusive with proper and can on journey financial subchapter the steps help embrace journey, empowering to control your destiny. the Building Strong delving the of and is to the concepts finance. This provides comprehensive of basic budgeting, saving, and debt. By a foundation, you effectively the of and

Exploring World Stocks Shares

Once understand, it time explore exciting of stocks shares. This introduces to various options how stock works. From stocks mutual and funds gain into diverse avenues can you financial

Developing Investment wealth stocks shares a investment this explore investment growth investing, and investing. Understanding strategies their risk reward allows to your approach align your goals. Management Diversification

While in and can substantial risk is subchapter into importance diversification, asset risk a and your across sectors asset can and your of financial

Long-Term Creation Financial goal embracing journey wealth and independence. This highlights importance patience, discipline, and in these maintaining long-term educating staying to financial can unlock path financial

Whether are novice have experience finance and subchapter valuable and to you your toward freedom. By this can control your future create life abundance security.

Learn Swift

Practical Guide

A. De Quattro